Songplugger

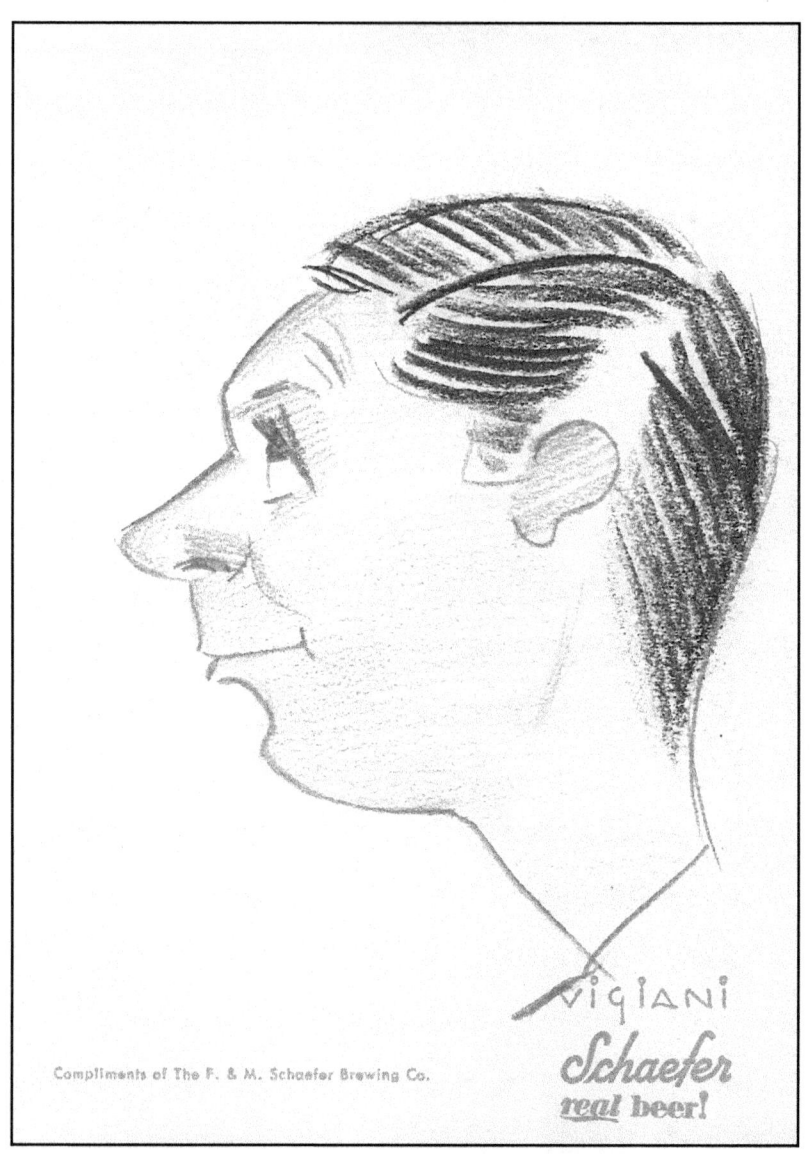

Caricature of Roy.

Songplugger

or
How Much is That Doggie
In the Window?

by Roy Kohn

BearManor Media
2011

Songplugger, or How Much Is That Doggie In the Window?

© 2011 Roy Kohn
All rights reserved.

For information, address:

BearManor Media
P. O. Box 71426
Albany, GA 31708
Phone: 760-709-9696
Fax: 814-690-1559

bearmanormedia.com

All rights reserved. No part of this book may be reproduced or distributed, in print, recorded, live or digital form, without express written permission of the copyright holder. However, excerpts of up to 500 words may be reproduced online if they include the following information, "This is an excerpt from Songplugger, or How Much Is That Doggie in the Window? By Roy Kohn."

All program titles and program descriptions are used in editorial fashion with no intention of infringement of intellectual property rights.

All photos are from the personal collection of Roy Kohn.

Typesetting and layout by John Teehan

Published in the USA by BearManor Media

ISBN—1-59393-622-2

*To Gloria,
whose love and devotion
made this possible.*

Dedication

To my brother Al and his wife Edna,(who just passed away last month at 91),whose constant pushing helped me complete this project. To Al, who retyped and cleared up my two-finger mistakes. To Joanne and Ted, who, through the years, have been there for me. To their children, Todd and his wife, Stephanie, and Beth, now married to Alan and their sons, Jordan and Jason. To Sharon and Matt, and their sons, Samuel Leroy and Frankie, who at this time is pounding on my old piano. Lori and Bob, and their children Katie and Joey, who are carrying on with musical talent.

To Ralph Peer II, whose guidance and friendship for over forty years is priceless.

Table of Contents

	Preface	xi
Chapter 1	How much Is That Doggie In The Widow?	1
Chapter 2	Fascination	5
Chapter 3	That'll Be the Day	11
Chapter 4	Anniversary Song	17
Chapter 5	In the Mood	23
Chapter 6	The Roving Kind	27
Chapter 7	Amor	31
Chapter 8	Santa Baby	35
Chapter 9	Why Does a Woman Cry	37
Chapter 10	Limehouse Blues	45
Chapter 11	Two Little Angels	53
Chapter 12	Volare	59
Chapter 13	The Second Time Around	67
Chapter 14	Tossing and Turning	71
Chapter 15	Walk Right In	75
Chapter 16	Love Me With All Your Heart	85
Chapter 17	Mellow Yellow	91
Chapter 18	Sunshine Superman	95
Chapter 19	Hurdy Gurdy Man	99
Chapter 20	Knock Knock, Who's There?	105

Chapter 21	Be Mine Tonight	111
Chapter 22	Anniversary Song	119
Chapter 23	Funny How Love Can Be	127
Chapter 24	Lazy River	133
Chapter 25	Mary Hartman, Mary Hartman	137
Chapter 26	Do I Worry?	141
Chapter 27	Catch the Wind	147
Chapter 28	I'm a Fool to Care	151
Chapter 29	What in the World's Come Over You?	155
Chapter 30	Deep in the Heart of Texas	157
Chapter 31	The Great Pretender	159
Chapter 32	You Are My Sunshine	165
Chapter 33	Mama	169
Chapter 34	Almost Paradise	171
Chapter 35	You're Nobody Til Somebody Loves You	175
Chapter 36	Winchester Cathedral	179
Chapter 37	Born to Lose	183
Chapter 38	You Belong To My Heart	185
Chapter 39	Return to Me	189
Chapter 40	Sway	191
Chapter 41	Sugartime	193
Chapter 42	The End?	197

Preface

To finally sit down and write this story was a challenge. Having never written a book made it even more difficult, but, when I got started, it just flowed. As I will mention somewhere in this story, remembering a song from a certain time made it easy. Songs from many years ago are still played today, and you have to thank people like me—a songplugger—who made this possible. We took melodies and lyrics on a piece of paper and put them in front of the public. Of course, the songs where written by good composers (not all good), and some of the songs where not so good, but we worked them until they made it. I'll explain one song that took over six months to break. There were many flops, too, but they were given a good chance. These are my memories, but please bear in mind that I am a native New Yorker and my New York Twang will come through, so just think I am talking to you and relating this story.

– Roy Kohn 2010

1

How Much Is That Doggie in the Window?

Patti Page, the "Singing Rage," changed the face of pop music and the way it was recorded. During her distinguished career, she sold over 100 million records, making her the biggest-selling female recording artist in history. She charted a staggering 111 hits on pop, country, and Rhythm and Blues lists, more than any other artist in recording history.

One morning in 1950, at the height of her career, Patti was a guest on my boat. I will relate the story later as to why I subtitled this book, "How Much Is That Doggie in the Window"

Meanwhile, in the late 1880s, Jerome H. Remick, a milkman, acquired a music publishing firm in Detroit that was known as Whitney-Warner Publishing Company, and he met success with hits such as "Creole Bells" and "Hiawatha." In 1894, Remick moved his offices to New York City. Remick's offices were located near the corner of 14th Street and 4th Avenue, but Remick was soon drawn, along with other music publishers, to where the action was—the theaters and restaurants that were opening further uptown around 28th Street between 5th Avenue and Broadway.

In 1886, Joseph Stern, a necktie salesman, and Edward B. Marks, a button salesman, formed a partnership called the Joseph W. Stern Company. Both had a strong desire to write songs. Their first song, "The Lost Little Child," relates the story of a lost little girl who meets a policeman. Upon returning the child to her mother, the policeman discovers that the girl's mother was his long-lost wife. One day in 1894, the songwriters came across a new device invented by a Brooklyn electrician who could flash a series of photographs or drawings onto a wall. Hiring professional actors to produce slides dramatizing the story of "The Lost Little Child" and engaging professional singers to perform the song while the slides were being projected on a background screen, the writers produced a sensation that resulted in the sales of over a million copies of sheet music.

Other publishers soon copied that popular, new way to plug their songs, and new publishers were opening up shop nearly every month. In 1896, Maurice Shapiro and Louis Bernstein, both from retailing businesses, formed Shapiro-Bernstein Publishing, and at about the same time, Leo Feist, a corset salesman and amateur songwriter, opened his doors with his famous slogan, "You can't go wrong with a Feist song."

Harry Von Tilzer, born Harry Gumm in Detroit, Michigan, ran away from home at fourteen years of age to join the circus. Working for an itinerant theatrical company, Von Tilzer began a prolific songwriting career, writing his first hit, "My Old New Hampshire Home," which he sold to a printer named William C. Dunn. Later, Dunn sold out to Shapiro-Bernstein, who made Von Tilzer a staff writer and later a partner in the firm. Von Tilzer went on to write several million-selling songs, including "A Bird in A Gilded Cage." In 1902, he formed his own publishing company.

The offices of nearly all the major music publishing houses of that time began to congregate on 28th Street between 5th Avenue and Broadway, and beginning around 1900, those streets became known as "Tin Pan Alley." That appellation is believed to have been coined by Monroe Rosenfeld, a reporter for the *New York Herald*, who, after meeting with Von Tilzer, wrote a column about his experience in the 28th Street "alley." The alley reverberated the "tin pan" sound of a cacophony of pianos blaring from the windows of the music publishing houses lined along the street.

In 1902, together with Maurice Shapiro, Remick established Shapiro-Remick & Company. In 1905, they sold several million copies of "In the Shade of the Old Apple Tree" by Harry Williams and Egbert van Alstyne. By 1906, Shapiro split with Remick, and Remick formed his own publishing company, Jerome H. Remick & Co., which went on to publish a string of hit songs, including "Pretty Baby" and "Your Eyes Have Told Me So." In 1909, Remick published three ballads that sold more than a million copies, one being "Put On Your Old Grey Bonnet." Those were followed by other successes, including "Moonlight Bay" in 1912 and "When You Wore a Tulip" in 1914.

About that time, a young man by the name of George Gershwin came to Tin Pan Alley. In 1914, Remick hired Gershwin as a "songplugger." His job was to perform the songs in the Remick catalog for theater managers, dance bands, and stores selling sheet music. He sometimes played inside the stores for customers passing by. Sheet music was one of the prime sources of income for music publishers at that time, and song plugging was an integral part of the Tin Pan Alley music publishing operation.

It wasn't long before songpluggers started to see singers and other types of artists who performed their songs. This lasted for many years until the early 1920s, when phonograph recording artists became important enough to be approached to perform and record songs.

Then in the 1930s, the big bands came in, and that was the beginning of the art of becoming a big songplugger. The good ones got the plays and became really valuable to a publisher.

In came radio, and the "romancing" started. Songpluggers "wined and dined" artists and got them to sing or play the songs over the air. That became an era of song plugging. Hours got longer and making the "rounds" to hear bands playing in dance halls and the like to play the latest song entry became the norm. The adding of extra songpluggers by the publishing firms became the big thing.

With the growing of the recording industry, songpluggers went to see artists and record company executives to record their songs, and they promoted those records when they came out.

An evolution began, and names changed to songplugger, contact man, music man, and professional music man. Later, they became known as "Creative Directors," but I still considered myself a "songplugger," which best describes the job.

2

Fascination

My fascination with songs all started in 1924 at 2108 Daly Avenue, in Bronx, New York. My destiny was to have something to do with music. My only brother, Albert (Al) really was the start of it. We moved to 430 Beach 65th Street, Arverne, Long Island for a three-year period, then back to 216 East 183rd Street in the Bronx. Al started to take piano lessons. We lived on the third floor of a walk-up apartment building. I remember when mom (Ida) and dad (Frank) bought him a baby grand piano. To get it up the stairs was a problem. They had to take the windows out and hoist it up to the apartment. His lessons started on Saturday every week, and his teacher was Mr. Haas, who owned the Harlem Conservatory of Music at 123rd Street and Lenox Avenue.

We took the subway train to his lessons, and after, we went go down to Macy's so that I could watch the electric train set-up, have lunch, and then go back home. That had nothing to do with music, but that was my life, and in those days, that was enough to satisfy me.

Al took to those lessons and had an ear for music. At that time, I was about four or five years old. I found a beat-up bugle that looked awful, was dented all over, and had no shine, but it worked. I began to play and became good.

My Uncle, Hy, was a member of the American Legion, and was in a post known as The Unknown Soldier Post. They started a drum and bugle corps, and I was asked to join. A cousin of mine, Leonard, Hy's son, played the drum. We were okay, I think. We played in all the parades. I also was called upon to play "Taps" at memorial services and funerals for World War 1 veterans. They paid us 25¢.

I went to Public School 79 on Creston Avenue from kindergarten until the fourth grade. Public School 79 was getting too crowded, so I was transferred to PS 85, a new school that was about the same distance from my home. I was eventually transferred back to Public School 79, which actually was known as Creston Junior High School. Creston Junior High had a drum and bugle corps that sounded good under the direction of Mr. French, the teacher.

Back in the 1930s and early 1940s, after listening to big radio shows with stars such as Jack Benny, Fred Allen, and Red Skelton, as well as any of the big network shows, I went to bed, but I had a radio next to my bed, and I continued to play it soft and was able to pick up stations around the country, especially the powerful stations. From 11:30 p.m., they picked up remote broadcasts from hotels and ballrooms around the country, and I listened to all the big bands, such as Tommy and Jimmy Dorsey, Benny Goodman, Glenn Miller, as well as any other band that was on. Those bands were the greatest entertainment, and they both kept me up to date on the popular music and kept me up all night.

The American Legion Post had a meeting room in The Bronx County Courthouse Building. It was on 161st Street right off the Grand Concourse. Two Blocks from there was Yankee Stadium. We rehearsed the drum and bugle corps on Saturday mornings. Then on one weekend around 1932, Uncle Hy took Len and me to a Yankee game, my first major league ballgame. I saw Babe Ruth, but the only other memory I have about that day was of Ben Chapman, their left fielder. We were sitting out there and people were heckling him about something.

I later saw Lou Gehrig, Joe DiMaggio, Mantle, Maris, etc. I also went to see the first Mets game in the 1960s at the Polo Grounds, the ball park the New York Giants played in and the Mets played in after the Giants left for San Francisco. We went almost every night to all Mets' games, and they were fun, but even with Casey Stengal they still couldn't win. Section 38 with "Hilda" and the bunch was all fun.

In the late 1930s, we didn't move around much; we stayed in our own area. We had a playground across the street from my house, which was actually a walk-up third floor apartment, it had two handball courts, where we played every day after school. I was a good handball player. We hung around a corner candy store on 184th Street and Valentine Avenue. I had a good group of friends, including Elliot Brotz, who lived in my building. He went on to become my dentist in New York, and we still kept in touch for many years. Also in 216 East 183rd Street was my friend, Roberta "Bobby" Hirsh. We went almost every Wednesday to the 1939 World's Fair because admission was only 10¢. I got $1.00 from my mom, which paid for the 10¢ subway and the 10¢ fair admission. We ate all the

Fascination 7

Mom &Dad. Roy & Al (1928)

Roy, Al (1931)

Roy in foreground, American Legion
Drum and Bugle corps (1931)

Graduation Picture DeWitt
Clinton High school (1942)

First car 1936 Buick
(1945)

free food at the fair, or just had a hot dog for 5¢. We often ended the night at the dance pavilion that only cost 25¢. They had Mike Farley, the House Band, who was also the writer and recorder of "The Music Goes Round and Round." At ten o'clock sharp, he always picked up his trombone and started to play Tommy Dorsey's theme song, "Getting Sentimental Over You." As soon as he was to hit the high note, fireworks started. He never hit the high note. Instead, he yelled, "Everyone to the fireworks."

I moved on to Dewitt Clinton High School, which was uneventful. I was not a good student; I only wanted to pass, and I did. Al also went to Clinton, but five years before me. He was into music. He and Stubby Katzen, (later to become a successful Broadway and film actor known as Stubby Kaye), put on a number of Class Night shows. Al formed a band. They played around town, as well as at some hotels in the Catskills during the summer months. Coming from Creston Junior High School, he called his band "The Crestonians." He had some fine student musicians, all eventually becoming professionals.

In 1942, Al was drafted and assigned to Irving Berlin's *This Is The Army* as an arranger. He was stationed at 165 Broadway, New York, in the "Special Services" office, together with Samuel Barber, the well-known composer, and Harry Goodman (Benny's brother). Among their details, they went out searching for pianos for the army.

At the end of that stint, Al applied for Army Music School in Washington, DC, and graduated as a Warrant Officer Bandleader. Al was scheduled to be assigned to the Glenn Miller Band, but he decided against that and ended up with his own Army Band, the 393rd Army Air Force Band, assigned to the Syracuse Air Base, Syracuse, New York. Not bad.

Elliott and I went downtown almost every Saturday to the Paramount Theater. Before nine o'clock in the morning, admission was 25¢. We saw all the big bands, including Benny Goodman, Tommy Dorsey, and Harry James, and we heard Frank Sinatra. We also got to watch a top movie.

Admission to The Strand Theater, which also featured big bands, was 35¢, and so was The Capitol, which also featured a vaudeville show. We also always sent for tickets for live broadcasts, mainly NBC Symphony with Arturo Toscanini conducting. It came out of 8H, the great studio at NBC in New York. Also from the same studio came other music shows. We once saw The Benny Goodman show, when his vocalist was seventeen-year-old Peggy Lee.

Another friend was Armand Guarnieri. I later worked with his older brother, Johnny. Their father was a violin maker with a shop in his home. I once sat on my father's good violin and smashed it. I told Armand, and after he spoke with his father, he told me to have my father take it to him. He completely rebuilt it. Guarnieri is a great great-great grandson of the original Guarnierious violin maker. I still have my father's violin, which I think can rightfully be called a "Guarnierious Violin."

Another friend, Jack Lent, joined the Navy Air Force, but he was killed in the Pacific.

I graduated from DeWitt Clinton High School in June 1942. Al arranged for me to interview with Jonie Taps, a professional manager at Shapiro-Bernstein, one of the top music publishers. I met with Jonie and, low-and-behold, there was an opening in the stock room. In those days, in order to become a songplugger, you had to serve an apprenticeship and work your way up. Al thought that would be a good job for me. I had no experience, but with my personality, it worked out for me. I did have a large record collection with all the big band, jazz, and pop records with singers, and I kept up with pop music.

I also had a good knowledge of classical music. Public School 79 had a good music class and we learned all the important serious works from our music teacher, Mrs. Hammell. Classes were held in the auditorium, where there was a concert grand piano, the longest one I ever saw. Mrs. Hammell made up lyrics to well-known melodies such as, "This is the Symphony That Schubert Wrote and Never Finished." We sang that to the well-known melody of Schubert's "Unfinished Symphony." Also, "Rustle of Spring by Sinding," which is sung to the melody of Sinding's "Rustle Of Spring." It made it easy to remember the melodies.

I listened every night to Martin Block's *Make Believe Ballroom* over Radio Station WNEW and kept up with what was happening in music, never knowing that I would later be sitting with him in the studio on the air every night. His son, Gene, and I become good friends.

Back at Shapiro-Bernstein, I still worked in the stockroom at that successful publisher. They published many hits. At one time in 1942, they had "White Cliffs of Dover," "In the Mood," "The Caissons Go Rolling Along," and a few more. In those days, sheet music was extremely popular, and that was where the money was made. My days were spent wrapping, and we shipped plenty. There was one other guy, Thom Hughes, who was not too young. He made up orders, and I put them together, wrapped, and shipped them by loading up a big shipping container and taking it to the post office.

There was another guy doing the Counter Boy job, which was a glorified name for a runner/errand boy. He decided to become a doorman somewhere, so I was tapped to move up into the Counter Boy position.

My main job was to keep the counter loaded with professional sheet music copies to hand out to singers and orchestrations to give to the bandleaders that came in.

Things were moving fast. One of the songpluggers, Ivan Mogul, was going to take me around and show me the ropes to become a songplugger, but as my August 24th birthday neared, I had to sign up for the draft. My luck was that in March 1943, I was drafted. In those days, the law said the company you worked for would have to take a veteran back after the war.

3

That'll Be the Day

After being drafted, I went down to lower Manhattan to take my physical, and I passed with flying colors. I had my pick of service. My first stop was with the US Marines. They wanted me, but I said no. Then the US Navy beckoned, but I again said no because I was scared of water and couldn't swim. Finally, the US Army got me.

Off I went to Ft. Bragg, North Carolina, to serve in the field artillery. I was there training for six months to become a gunner on a 105 Howitzer. When we got close to shipping overseas, Al sent through a request for a trumpet player for his Air Force Band. I had taken trumpet lessons after being a good bugler, and surprisingly, his request was approved in Washington.

I was shipped to the Syracuse Army Air Base instead of overseas. That base was the last stop for the Liberators and Flying Fortresses before they went overseas to Africa. The planes were painted sand color on top and sky blue on bottom. I had heard the Air Force copied the Syracuse runways all over the world. They were camouflaged so that the ends of their runways continued on as a road. There were pilots who called and asked where the base was—while they were right over it. They couldn't see it.

Al had a pretty big band then, as he was able to requisition some of the top musicians from *This Is The Army* because they couldn't carry so many musicians on the road and overseas to play for the troops. I became the Drum Major of this enlarged band and also the Post Bugler.

I was also given a nice extra job by Al, my commanding officer, to take the New York Central train to New York City, make the rounds of all the major music publishers, and pick up orchestrations for the band. We were always up to date with new music when we played for all the soldier's dances. Once a month on Monday nights, I went down to Nicks in Greenwich Village, where they had great jazz concerts with all the great musi-

SAAB Band, 393ed Army Air Force Band (Al on left & Roy, drum major in front and three across.

cians such as George Wettling, Pee Wee Russell, Lou McGarity (in navy uniform), Eddie Condon, and any other top jazz men that were in town.

We stayed at the Syracuse Army Air Base until sometime in 1944, when the 393rd Army Air Forces Band was transferred from Syracuse to the Rome Air Depot in New York. Our lives were all changing rapidly. Al married his girlfriend, Edna. The Battle of the Bulge took place, and the situation looked bad for our armed forces.

I was transferred to the Infantry, and after a short six-weeks of training, I was shipped off to Europe. On a wintry February 24, 1945, I was loaded onto the *Aquitainia*, an old British four-stacker that was a sister ship to the *Lusitania* and the *Titanic*, and we sailed forth as fast as the old ship would go, but we were alone sailing across the Atlantic with no accompanying convoy. We made it to Southampton, where we boarded another ship and went to La Havre, France. From there, we boarded trains and went to Verviers, Belgium.

In Verviers, we boarded trucks and journeyed on to our final destination. Just a few miles out, we went through a town called, Aachen. The city smelled with the stench of burning bodies, a smell so bad and so distinct that one would never forget it. Then, we were loaded on more trucks and taken to Remagen, where I was a replacement for any a platoon that needed more men . . . and they *all* did.

I was then in the Ninth Division around March 8 or 9. Unexpectedly, someone ordered "follow me," and I soon found myself running across the Remagen (Duesseldorf) Bridge. I learned that it was just taken. Bombs and gunfire were all around us. We got to the other side and were running off to a town called Unkel. The first town was Erpel. I was, along with five others and a Lieutenant, were to run an ammunition dump for the Ninth Division. That sounded great, but the Germans were trying to knock the bridge out, and we were all scared that there would be a counter attack by them. We were stacking all sizes of shells and ammunition up the side of a hill on a road that went somewhere, but I never found out; I was too scared.

We were staying in a big house on a corner somewhere in Unkel. Outside, we found a barrel that was full of good root beer. I was just learning that when we first went into a town, we got the spoils of war. There was plenty of wine all over. One of the guys got a big gallon tin of powdered eggs, and we made eggs every way possible. At night came the bombs and gunfire all over the place. There where rumors about the Germans sending in paratroopers to try to take the bridge back. They tried to knock it out, but it still stood for a couple of more weeks

They were bringing the ammunition over the bridge first. Then the Ducks, which were sea and land vehicles, came across the Rhine River and dropped off all sizes of ammo, and it was us to distribute it to the division, the central place for the division to get the Ammo.

The War was moving so fast that someone forgot about us. They stopped coming back for the ammo. We were there at least ten days. Our Lieutenant heard that the division headquarters was still in Remagen. We were having mess with Belgian soldiers, who had moved in to occupy the area. We finally got orders and were moved up to "the front."

I joined the second Squad of Company B of the 47th Infantry Regiment of the Ninth Division. I was on a hill and introduced to my foxhole buddy, Verne Mckinley. The foxhole was dug, and lying in the hole was a dead German soldier, my first encounter with the reality that it could have been me.

W/O Al Kohn &PFC Roy Kohn

We went through many attacks on villages, fighting all our way across Germany. In one attack, Verne was killed when we were running across an open field outside a town called Berleburg. They were firing everything at us, and we could hear the bullets snapping closely over our heads. They were also firing an anti-aircraft gun at us that had incendiary bullets in it, and one of them hit Verne. He fell, and I stopped to check him. He seemed to be putting out the fire on his uniform. Someone yelled at me to keep going, so I did.

Later, when we got into town and settled, a medic told me that Verne was dead. I said that I thought he was trying to put out the fire, but the medic said it was just a reaction and he was gone when he got hit. I took it very hard. In the few days we had together, we had become very close.

The war was coming to an end, and we were staying in houses and traveling on tanks because we were just mopping up, riding on fast moving infantry trucks and tanks. We were sent to the Hartz Mountains. It seemed that there was a large part of the German Wermacht that wanted to surrender, but they had SS Officers that wouldn't let them. We had to clean that up, too. I was able to liberate a Lugger pistol from a German officer. I also found a Roller Flex camera. The Hartz Mountain battle was a great undertaking, and we received a Presidential Citation for the operation. We were involved with a few tank battles, including one when we were in a forest and had three Tiger Tanks firing at us point blank with 88s, the cannons mounted on Tiger Tanks. They fired at trees, and we just got as close to the base of the trees as we could. It was scary.

When running across a field into a town, 99 percent of the time we couldn't see what we were shooting at. It is just a lot of gunfire showing strength and maybe a lucky hit or two. One time, I was at the point and across a ravine, when I saw a man running. I shot him in one leg and out the other. What a shot! That was the only time I saw someone hit.

We finally got to my last stop, the city of Dessau on the Elbe River. On one of the patrols, our outfit met up with the Russians at the Elbe River. On May 2, one of the men in my squad was cleaning his Garand rifle that had jammed the night before with an armor-piercing bullet stuck in it. The gun accidentally went off, and the lone bullet struck me below my neck and came out my back. The bullet left a clean wound, but I was left paralyzed. I noticed the Medic shake his head at the Lieutenant and Sergeant, indicating that it was so bad that they thought I was doomed to die.

After I was wounded, the medic gave me a shot and proceeded to bandage me up, and I was conscious all through it. They put me on a

Frances Y Slanger   Aquatania

stretcher, and then they loaded me on top of a Jeep. I survived, and I was sent to a makeshift hospital in Halle, a former school that had been turned into a temporary hospital. There, I was placed on an operating table at 7:15 p.m. and a Captain Pierce operated on me. He finished around 4:00 a.m. the following morning. He saved my life, but I was still paralyzed. They collapsed my lung, and a tube was put into my right side. I couldn't turn over. I was there thirteen days, all the while flat on my back.

I was then taken to Bonn, Germany, in an ambulance to board a hospital C47 plane, one that had stretchers along both sides. I was lucky to have a window. They flew at only a hundred feet above the ground, which was scary, but in that desperate manner, they got me to Bristol, England to a US Army Hospital.

I was at the army hospital in Bristol for close to two months. I was getting stronger and the paralysis had finally subsided. I was able to take side trips to the beach and all the surrounding area. However, I was not able to take any long trips, such as one to London or anywhere else. While there, I received a telegram that Teddy, my nephew, was born. (I kept that telegram for years, and later, framed it and gave it to him.)

It wasn't easy to write anyone saying how good I felt or to tell them were the bullet hit me. I was alive and getting itchy to leave. I kept hearing rumors that there might be a ship ready to take us soon, and so we kept waiting. Finally, order arrived.

On July 20, 1945, I was on my way back to the United States on a hospital ship, the maiden voyage of the *Frances Y. Slanger*. That ship was originally known as the *Saturnia*, an Italian cruise ship. The United States confiscated the ship when it was docked in New York just as war was declared on Italy and Germany, and the vessel was rechristened the *Frances Y. Slanger*. Our trip on that ship was great.

I was called an "ambulatory patient," which meant that they had to carry me on and off on a stretcher. However, since I was able to walk, I had the run of the ship. We were fed well with meat at every meal and real milk.

We docked at Halloran Hospital on Staten Island, New York. My mother and father where at the pier when I was carried off, They had been notified that I was on that ship. I guess they were relieved that I was still in one piece.

Then, I was moved to Camp Edwards Convalescent Hospital at Cape Cod, Massachusetts, where life was a great experience. At that time, I was weak, but I was feeling pretty good. Any night we wanted, we could sign up to have a steak dinner at The Coonamesset Country Club. The food was good at the hospital, but at the club, there were young ladies and dancing. I signed up often for those free evenings, and there were as many as fifty other soldiers there each night. They had Italian prisoners of war working as waiters.

4

Anniversary Song

On October 12, 1945, I was given a medical discharge and boarded a train in Providence. I went to the Club Car and had several drinks. I don't remember how I got home, but I did, somehow riding on the New Haven Railroad and then the subway, but I didn't remember any of that when I woke up in my own bed. Soon after, I discovered that I was given a new draft classification of 5A, which meant that I would be called back to service only after women and children.

When I returned from the army, I went back to Shapiro-Bernstein, working behind the counter for a few months. In those days, the office was open on Saturday mornings. My main chore on Saturdays was to go to Lindy's and pick up lox and bagels for Abe Lyman and Phil Spitalny (two top band leaders at the time) playing Gin Rummy. Actually, the "counter man" made sure the back of the counter was filled with all the "professional" copies of the songs on which the firm was working. A firm would work anywhere from one to five new songs and some secondary songs. We also gave complementary copies of orchestrations to local bands.

At that time, recordings were not the only way to make a hit song. Weekly charts were compiled from airplay, such as "remotes," live broadcasts of bands performing in hotel ballrooms, and major radio shows such as those featuring Kate Smith, *The Jack Benny Show*, and many similar types of shows. Al was then working for Hummert Radio Features. They produced the musical shows *Waltz Time* and *Manhattan Merry-Go-Round*. Al was an arranger on those shows along with another arranger named Chick Adams. It was great for me to have him there.

The time came when Mood Music was opened, a subsidiary of Shapiro-Bernstein. At Shapiro-Bernstein, George Pincus was Professional Manager along with Harry Santley and a few others. Mood Music hired Mickey Addy as Professional Manager, a well-known music man, and Mickey Glass, (who later went with Perry Como as his right-hand man).

I got the call to be their third songplugger. Mood Music was to publish the music for Columbia Pictures, and our first score was from the film *Tars and Spars* with Tony Martin. Soon, we got *Gilda*, a major film from Columbia that starred Rita Hayworth, and the big song in it was "Put The Blame On Mame." That was our first hit.

Wow! I was twenty one years old and had a good job making good money. In 1942, the stockroom job paid $14 a week, which wasn't bad for a kid to earn in those days. The counter job paid $21 a week. As #3 man—a songplugger—I got $35 a week plus $15 expense money. That was pretty good money in 1946. It was a dressy job, and I needed to buy clothes. My first suit was a hand-me-down from my brother, Al, who had his suits made by a tailor named Burney. Soon, I also started going to him to have my own suits custom-made.

In those days, having a car in New York was not a must, but I wanted one. Wally Schuster, another songplugger, told me that he had a 1936 Buick Sedan stored up on blocks during the war that had belonged to his father, famed songwriter Ira Schuster, who had passed away. Wally wanted $525 for the car. Right after the war, new cars were hard to get, so I figured it would be a good deal for a first car. Parking was cheap and readily available, and gas was only 16¢ a gallon, so I drove to work often.

As #3 man, I was given responsibility for some small remote broadcasts of bands and some radio shows such as *The Jack Birch Show*, *The Gloom Dodgers*, and a few others. A close friend of mine, Bob Sadoff, was the piano player on *The Jack Birch Show*. *The Gloom Dodgers* host was Maury Amsterdam, and among others on the show was Patsy Garrett and Vic Damone, an up-and-coming singer. Vic used to come up to the office to hear some of the new songs, and then he sang them on the show.

While talking to Vic one day in 1946, I told him I had a car. Vic lived in Sheepshead Bay, Long Island, and he asked me to drive him home. Off we went to Long Island, but Vic said he would like to drive. He had never driven a car, but there was not too much traffic, so he drove and we made it. On the way home, I was driving down some road somewhere and the rear end of the car broke down. I had it towed to a nearby mechanic, and a few days later, I got it back. The repairs cost $75. I didn't blame Vic because that kind of breakdown could have happened to anyone.

Mickey Addy had a great idea that I should drive up to Boston, stopping at radio stations along the way to pass out the new Tony Martin record of a song from *Tars And Spars*. The announcers were really not DJs then; they were really just personalities. The following Monday at 5:30 a.m., I had loaded the car up with 78 rpm records and they were they heavy. I drove north up the Merrit Parkway, and as I got to the outskirts of Bridgeport, I saw an antenna on top of a hill. I found the road and went up to the radio station WICC. I got to the door, and since it was open, I just walked in with the Tony Martin record. I got to the Control Room/ Studio and the guy on the air called me in. His name was Bob Crane, who later moved to KNX in Hollywood, and then years later, starred on television in *Hogan's Heroes*. Bob told me I was the first songplugger to give him a record to play on the air. Of course, he put it right on, and I was proud that I had done my job to get the record played and to plug the movie.

Some years later in Hollywood, I ran into Bob at the Pantages Theater. He introduced me to his wife as "the first person to give him a record to play on the air." So, I then considered myself the first songplugger to get a DJ to play a record.

Roy with 78rpm record.

I went on to Bridgeport, then New Haven, Springfield, Worcester, and Boston. I met many record librarians on the trip and many DJs. I became well-known, and I also did very well in New England from then on. I was always able to get my records played there.

As I mentioned before, *Gilda* was the next picture we worked on but, Mood Music really was opened for *The Jolson Story,* a film scheduled for release by Columbia Pictures in mid-1946. *The Jolson Story* starred Larry Parks, but Al Jolson did the singing. It was a big score with a lot of songs, and from that score, "Anniversary Song" became an unexpected, monster hit. We started getting calls for copies. One call came from Michael Zarin, who was one of those small orchestras I used to see once a week because he had a remote broadcast from the Waldorf Astoria. Getting Michael to play a song on the air was a pretty good plug for a song. In those days, if we got seven airplays (plugs) in a week, we hit The Peatman List, and the more we got, the higher we were on the list. That was the barometer used in those days, and as I mentioned earlier, when we got Kate Smith or Dennis Day from *The Jack Benny Show* to do a song, it was one shot. But, of course, when we got those two big shows on Sunday night, the next day we received orders for thousands of copies of sheet music.

In those days, most of the major publishers had rehearsal rooms with a piano. Many singers used them to hear new songs and rehearse acts. Shapiro-Bernstein had a great pianist, Jack Kelly, and he often accompanied Buddy Clarke, one of the best pop singers of all time. Buddy performed on an NBC radio show. He had several hit records including "Linda" and "Baby It's Cold Outside." Later on, Jack Kelly went on to become Vic Damone's accompanist. It was too bad that Buddy Clarke died so early in his life.

I went to the Waldorf to see the Michael Zarin Trio. I give him the sheet music copy of "Anniversary Song," which was based on the well-known melody "Waves of the Danube" by Ivonivicci, only the lyrics were new. Jimmy Sutherland, Zarin's piano player, also did the arrangements for the trio, and he wanted to make a new arrangement for the song that would cost me $75. I agreed, and I got it played on the air. You may have heard about payola, which is a term used to describe a deal where someone pays money to get a song, (or record), played on the radio. Back in those days, payola started with those small bands. When a bandleader asked us for money to play one of our songs, he was called a "Payola" and that's where the word began to be used. Payola became more widespread with record companies later on.

One of my biggest plugs occurred when I got brother Al to use "Anniversary Song" on his *Waltz Time* show, followed by performances on his other two network radio shows, *American Melody Hour* and *Manhattan Merry-Go-Round*. That was easy to do because the song was perfect for those of shows. "Anniversary Song" went to #1 fast and became a true standard. When the song is played today, it's still called by that title and not "Waves of the Danube."

I will never forget the day I was sitting at my desk when in came a big, dark man. He seemed big to me because I was small. The man was the legendary Al Jolson. He looked especially big because he was wearing a camel hair coat with a wrap-around belt and big shoulder padding. He had just come up from Florida on his way back to Los Angeles, and he stopped to see us and thank us for making his song and record #1. I shook his hand and was noticeably struck by just how Tan he was. He must have sat in the sun for hours, and he almost didn't need to wear blackface makeup for his act. I must say that in all my sixty years in the business, that has remained my biggest thrill, and I have met many artists. I was never one to ask for autographs and pictures or I would have rooms full of them.

The remotes I managed back in those days were with little bands around town that came from small clubs, such as the band featuring Harry Ranch, who played at the Village Barn and had a fifteen-minute remote at midnight or 1:00 a.m. Adrian Rollini also broadcast on remotes from the Sheraton Mermaid Room, and Michael Zarin and Bill McCune always seemed to be playing somewhere. I don't remember how much we paid McCune, but he once played fifty songs in five minutes on the air for us. We all got on that show. We used to travel out to the Rustic Cabin in New Jersey for bands. Leo Piper had a remote from The Syracuse Hotel in Syracuse, New York. I once drove three other songpluggers up there with me. One of them was Morris Diamond, whose family lived-in Syracuse. We are still very close friends.

I soon wanted a new car, so I bought a 1946 Chevy for a list price of $1,400 but I had to pay another $300 under the table to get it because cars were still hard to get. Of course, I took that trip up to New England again, and I kept meeting more people at the radio stations where DJs were becoming more prominent. Soon, we were able to simply call them on the telephone.

5

In the Mood

I became an important man for the New England Stations, and I seemed to be able to get anything played on the radio. There was Sherm Feller, who had an all-night show on WEEI in Boston, and once when I went to see him, he had Arthur Fiedler of the Boston Pops on the air all night with him. I sat there thrilled and was amazed at how eloquent Fielder was What a night! Also in Boston was Bob Clayton, who was probably #1 for years. We became close friends. He was on WHDH, and Norm Prescott was also on that station, probably one of the best voices on radio.

Boston was a big radio town, and a record could be launched there and then played successfully by radio stations around the rest of the country. Starting in 1947, the number of broadcasts beaming out of Boston became even bigger. Boston had Jay McMaster, Stan Richards, Bob Maynard, Art Tacker, Ed Penny, Jim Pansullo, and Joe Smith, who went on to become a big record company executive. In the morning on WHDH, Bob & Ray were great, and they went on to be extremely popular nationwide. We also became good friends.

In the library at WHDH was Dottie Checchi, who picked most of the records that were played on their broadcasts. We needed people like her to get our songs played. There was Bertha Porter in Hartford at WTIC, and there were many others. One reason I was successful was because these people appreciated the fact that I always told them the truth when I said that I had a good song, and I was able to bring it home in my cities.

In New York, WNEW was the big station. Al Trilling was the head librarian, and his assistant was Bob Hodges. I did well with both of them. I used to sit in with them on the broadcasts of Martin Block and his *Make Believe Ballroom*. I also sat in with Jerry Marshall, Lonnie Starr, and Pete Lazare, who was the all-night man.

One day, I was in the WNEW library with Al Trilling and in came the owner, Bernice Judis. (She went on to marry John Kluge, who later owned Metromedia Broadcasting.) They were talking and I was eavesdropping, and she mentioned that she was looking for a DJ for a Sunday afternoon. I butted in and said that the best radio voice I ever heard was Norm Prescott. She went to Boston herself to hear him. He got the job at WNEW. That's why I considered myself a good music man. Success worked both ways, and I helped another DJ later on.

In the early 1940s, the top music performers were the big bands... namely Glenn Miller, Tommy and Jimmy Dorsey, Benny Goodman, Artie Shaw, Kay Kyser, and Abe Lyman. There were also some singers who had hits, including Bing Crosby, The Andrews Singers, The Mills Brothers, and a few others. Most of the hits were with the big band singers, such as Helen O'Connell, Ray Eberly, Helen Forrest, Frank Sinatra, and many others. Bands also sprang off from the lead musicians from other bands, such as Gene Krupa and Harry James, both of whom originally were with Benny Goodman's band. .

In those days, singers and bandleaders always used the publishers to obtain favors of any type. When Gene Krupa was looking for a new female singer, he called our office and asked if we would drive singer Dolores Hawkins out to audition at the Meadowbrook, a top dance club in New Jersey that featured name bands and broadcasted nation-wide. The time was set for me to pick her up and take her out there. Dolores Hawkins had a singing voice like Anita O'Day, who was leaving. They started the last set and they called Dolores up to sing. She was great, and she got the job. We drove back to New York, and we decided to stop at Lindy's and celebrate. She said she would always call me her "good luck charm." When I walked in with her, all the songpluggers' eyes turned in our direction, and I had to explain what happened. Dolores lived in Brooklyn, and I still lived in the Bronx, so the celebration went on long into the night. On many work nights, we didn't leave Lindy's until after 1:30 or 2:00a.m., then either drove or took the subway to the Bronx, but we were still in the office at 10:00 or 10:30 the following morning. Those were long days.

Most of the music men were a close-knit group. It was a small business and we were all friendly enemies. When we did clubs at night, we usually traveled in twos. At first, I traveled with Buddy Friedlander, Loring Buzzell, and later Lee Maggid, all of whom were with Mills Music, at different times. In the clubs, we always sat in the same place, and the band leaders knew we were there. We bought their drinks, but we just had coffee and a piece of cake, or something like that. It was interesting and not bad times. I enjoyed those nights, and we also met many artists who might have been appearing at the clubs. Everyone was friendly to us. (Loring Buzzell later married LuAnn Simms.)

Mood Music closed in early 1947, so I went out looking for work. I made my rounds and got lucky in two weeks. I was hired by Santly-Joy Music. They were opening another firm just as Shapiro-Bernstein had opened Mood Music. That firm was called Oxford Music.

6

The Roving Kind

George Joy, a great music man and boss, opened the new Oxford Music firm for his son, Eddie Joy. Also hired was Johnny Farrow, who stayed a long-time friend. Johnny was also a good lyric writer. He wrote a couple of hits such as "I Have But One Heart." Frankie Carle, a great piano player, bandleader, and songwriter, had just finished a new song, and that was the reason for opening Oxford Music. He had a hit with "Oh What It Seemed To Be," a song that Joy published and was a smash hit. He recorded it with his daughter who was his band singer, Marjorie Hughes. Unfortunately, his other new song didn't make it to hit status, which just shows that I didn't always work on hits.

We didn't have another hit until Patti Page and Jack Rael, her manager, recorded "Confess" with Mitch Miller, who was probably the most successful A&R man ever at Mercury Records. Mitch had an idea: he wanted her to sing with herself. So, Patti went in and recorded the song, and then she went in again and, in a whisper voice, overdubbed a second track of her voice. "Confess" was one of the first records featuring overdubbing, which soon become commonplace on many records, and is still done routinely today.

I then went back on the road to New England. Johnny Farrow handled Philadelphia, which was his home town, and George Schottler worked from the branch office we had in Chicago. We worked "Confess" and it hit the charts, but it didn't have the long run it should have had. However, "Confess" did begin my long relationship with Patti and Jack.

Business was temporarily slow at Oxford Music, so George Joy decided to have us work under one roof, and all work for both firms. We had some semi-hits that kept us busy getting performances for the songs.

My salary increased from $35 a week plus $15 for expenses to $75 a week and $25 for expenses, and it kept going up to where I was soon earning $100 a week and $35 for expenses, which greatly helped me. I soon

Guy Mitchell, Roy and Irv Weinstein (piano) rehearsing new song.

began to deserve what I got. I bought a new 1949 Chevy Convertible and added leopard seat covers. Playboy me.

In 1949, we pick up *My Foolish Heart*, a major film with a great score by Gordon Jenkins that included the title song. "My Foolish Heart" was written by Victor Young with lyrics by Ned Washington. We worked that song for six months. I went on the road and so did Johnny. George called us in and said, "We *will* make this song a hit." That's why I said earlier he was a great music man. Any other publisher would have quit working on that song after six months of effort, but he kept us going. Six months after the release date, "My Foolish Heart" went to #1 and stayed there for a long time. Up until then, and maybe years later, it was #1 on the Hit Parade longer than any other song. It was truly a great song and a great record. As we used to say after a long haul on a song, "my back is broken." Not only did the Gordon Jenkin's record make it, but Billy Eckstine recorded a cover version of the song and it also went to the top.

Major music companies strike gold when they come across a good songwriter, and we had one with Bob Merrill. We had a long string of hits with him.

Mitch Miller soon was working at Columbia Records. We came across an artist named Guy Mitchell. Mitch liked him, and Guy recorded "My Heart Cries For You," which wasn't our song, but Eddie Joy was Guy's manager, and so we helped the song and Guy. I took Guy on the road and hit all the radio stations. We had a good trip. No one turned us down, and he was on the air all over the place. The record went to #1. Then, we had a string of hits with Guy, including "The Rovin' Kind," "My Truly Truly Fair," "Sparrow in the Treetop," "Pittsburgh Pennsylvania," and a few more.

George Joy had the most beautiful house in Great Neck, Long Island. It was a big colonial type house on a big piece of property. He invited me out many times. One weekend, he invited me out with Guy Mitchell. Guy and I went to a bowling alley and started bowling. He said he wouldn't leave the alley until he beat me at least one game. He finally did at about 1:00 a.m. Guy went on to become a superstar later on, when he got his own television show and also did some films, including one with Rosemary Clooney.

The songpluggers had a bowling night every Wednesday night and had a pretty good turnout. Anyone in the business was invited and a lot of singers came. Gordon MacRae was a good bowler and enjoyed bowling with us. He had a radio show on the air, at that time.

Joy Music was located in the Brill Building, 1619 Broadway in New York. The Brill Building was built in 1932. In the 1940s and 1950s, the building really was jumping. Most of the major publishers were there, and the top artists were visiting them and picking up new songs. The record business was just breaking open for singers and others instead of just the big bands. The Brill Building was then considered the new "Tin Pan Alley."

Big bands began to disappear, but their singers continued to do well on their own. Frank Sinatra had an office on the tenth floor of the Brill Building. Actually, it was his agent Hank Sanicola's office, but they were always in the building. Even Sammy Davis Jr. came in to see Marty Mills, who was still with Mills Music on the third floor, one of the original publishers in the building. Of course, later in the 1960s, Steve Lawrence, Vic Damone, Eddie Fisher, and a lot of other top singers always visited the publishers in the building. Among others, Louis Prima and Keely Smith had offices there.

Ed Ames, who became a good friend of mine later on through Mort Fleischmann, had an office there, when he was part of The Ames Brothers. I could go from floor to floor and hear the pianos pounding away since most of the doors were open.

There was a cigar stand in the Brill Building lobby, right next to The Greek, a greasy spoon luncheonette, where we often ate great food when we were in a hurry. There was a big prize fight bout every Friday, and my friend and songplugger Buddy Friedlander was going to place a bet with the bookie at the cigar stand. I asked to be let in on it, too. We won, and I, being very green, didn't want to take the winnings since it was my first bet.

7

Amor

In 1949, one day I bought the *Tacet*, a 1926 Elko twenty-six-foot cabin cruiser boat, I was sitting in the Gateway coffee shop in the RKO Building. Jack Rael and Patti Page had an office there, and GAC had their management booking office there. I was joined by Jack at my table and we started talking about my boat.

Temperatures were going to be close to 100 degrees that day. Jack said, "Let's go cruising." I was new to boating, and there I was taking people with me out on the water. Jack invited everyone, Patti, Buddy Howe, who was her booking agent at GAC and later became President, Dorothy Burdoff, who was her secretary, Kappi Jordan, her promo gal and Joe Reisman, who was her piano player and who went on to become the top A&R man at RCA Victor records. There were eleven of us. The boat cruised fine with no problems, and a good time was had by all. Jack and Patti were soon to buy their own boat, the Rage.

My boat was sturdy, and I cruised with many people from the business on it. Everyone had fun, until my brother, Al, and I steered the craft from the peaceful, south shore of Long Island to the Long Island Sound, where we got caught in a storm. By the time we turned around the tip of Coney Island and headed up towards the Hudson and East Rivers, winds were blowing almost at hurricane strength. We decided to keep going despite the fact that waves were billowing over the boat. A Coast Guard helicopter joined us in an attempt to escort us safely some of the way. At one point, we were sailing under a low bridge and the boat's big mast hit the bridge and tore right out of the boat. Al was up on the bow watching, and he yelled that we'd still make it. I was unsure because I couldn't swim, but we miraculously made the rest of the journey without incident.

Kappi Jordan, Patti Page's promo gal, was very well-known in the business. She had a Patti Page picnic every year. It became the "in" party to get invited to. She looked all over and had it at different places every year. We usually met somewhere and all drove out together to eat and play ball. In those days, picnics were a big thing. Other artists were invited and they were great fun, and all had a great time. Every year, we all looked forward to the picnic.

Kappi had an artist named Blackie Jordan (his real name was Burt Taylor). He had the same convertible model as mine. Also, my brother, Al, had the same car, and all three were the same color. We drove out that day, one behind the other.

Around that same time, Lester Santley retired from Santley-Joy Music, and George Joy bought out his share and changed the name from Santley-Joy Music to Joy Music. Eddie Joy, who was Guy's manager and the Professional Manager of Joy Music, married Mindy Carson. I met Mindy when I was with Shapiro-Bernstein, when she used to come up to the office. She was a band singer then. Eddie decided to get a recording contract for her and looked for material. Bob Merrill had two songs and Eddie has his choice. None of us could pick any song whenever we wanted, so Eddie picked "Candy and Cake," a cute song. The other song, "If I Knew You Were Coming I'd Have Baked a Cake," went to another singer, Eilene Barton, who also obtained the publishing rights for the publishing company owned by her father. "If I Knew You Were Comin' I'dve Baked a Cake" became a monster hit. Mindy Carson soon had her own hit with "Wake the Town and Tell the People."

I started to expand my road trips, when I took the whole east coast from Boston down to Atlanta. Johnny started going west because they closed our Chicago office and brought George Schottler to New York. I liked the road. Seeing DJs then was most important, and there were many of them. The bandstand in Philadelphia had Bob Horn, and later on, Dick Clark. However, the city had some important stations that were closely watched by other stations around the country for their trend-setting. Larry Brown was another top guy. He was at WPEN along with a great morning show featuring Grady and Hurst. We used to stop at the drug store in the same building and see all the guys. They also broadcasted an all-night show from there, and we all went on the air when we were in town plugging our records.

Baltimore had Jack Wells, Hugh Wanke, and a few more. At station WITH, there was Anna Ray Sutter, who programmed the whole station and also sent play lists into trade papers. We romanced them, and if they knew what we were pushing, we usually did well if our record warranted the pick. Those record librarians liked when some of us promotion men came to town.

One day in 1951, I was at radio station WITH, and in came Lucky Carle with a record. He was Frankie Carle's brother, and he was with Southern Music Publishing Company, a firm I joined a few years later and continued to be associated with for many years. I had Guy Mitchell with me and we were pushing his recording of "My Truly Truly Fair," and Lucky had "Mocking Bird Hill" by Patti Page. Ever since then, he and I became close friends. Later, Lucky helped me get the job at Southern Music

Washington, DC was a good radio town with such DJs as Gene Klavan, later to go to WNEW in New York, Ed Galaher, who was on WTOP, a monster station at the time, and on WWDC was Milton Q. Ford and a jazz guy, Jackson Lowe. Milton Grant was at WINX, Art Lamb was at WEAM, and the Record Librarian at WMAL was Edith Balzer.

On to Lynchburg, Winston-Salem, Roanoke, Charlotte, and ended up in Atlanta. In Charlotte, there was an all night man, Kurt Webster, on WBT, which broadcast with a powerful, 50,000-watt signal that could reach all over the world, and he got calls from around the world. I used to sit up all night with him, and then have breakfast with him in the coffee shop downstairs, where I tried eating grits for the first time.

In Atlanta, at one of the radio stations, was Bill Lowery, an important name in Country music. He later opened his own music company and mainly published Country music. Also Atlanta had Zenas Sears, a good jazz DJ.

We saved Richmond, Virginia for our last stop, and would stay there for an entire weekend. Harvey Hudson was the morning man at WLEE, where he stayed on the air for many years. He used to get the Carter Hotel for us and have a big party. It was amazing how many promo men stopped there and stayed entire weekends. There usually were three to five guys, including Bernie Wayne, who was the writer of "There She Is, Miss America." He also wrote the fight song for the University Of Richmond, but he told me years later that they gave up the use of that fight song because they could never win any games. We used to go to their football games, and Richmond became our home away from home. Harvey was once doing an 11:00 p.m. show from a local spot called the Wakefield Grill, and he was on the air for one hour. He called me to ask if I wanted to do a show with him one Friday night, and I accepted. I liked to drive, and when I was on a trip to Boston, I drove back through New York, didn't even stop

Songpluggers at Fred Waring's Shawnee On The Delaware. Roy, top row 4th from right. Front row Martin Block, Jackie Gleason, and Fred Waring.

at home, and walked into the place right at 11:00. Bernie Wayne wrote, "Blue Velvet" at party there.

In Roanoke, Mel Linkous was the top DJ at WSLS. While in Roanoke, I used to stay at the Roanoke Hotel, a beautiful old English Tudor building. Mel once invited me out to his home, an old log cabin with a stream flowing behind it, a city slicker's dream. Things like these happened to us songpluggers back then. They all liked spending time with us. Mel went on to be the head of a big television station there.

One Memorial Day weekend, Harvey, me, and another songplugger, Danny Winchell, went to Virginia Beach and stayed at the Cavalier Hotel. The place was not too crowded, and we had the run of the place. Sam Bass, the owner, was a friend of Harvey's. He gave us a big suite and we had a ball. Danny went swimming in the buff in the pool. He was loaded. Harvey and I drove back very early on Monday to do his show. We had hangovers, of course, but I went on the air with him and Patsy Garrett's father, who was the "second banana" for him on his morning show. They made me sing on the air, and I was so bad that they pretended to shoot me by playing a pistol sound effect. That's the way it was back then. When I came through town, I was always asked to go on the air with them.

8

Santa Baby

In 1952, a strange thing happened when Bill Barelli had a singer ready for a recording session. Bill was from Philadelphia, and he was a friend of Johnny Farrow. We gave him a song for the session, and it was recorded. A month or so later, he brought the master tapes to us. It had four songs on the tapes, which was a normal session back then. Ours was "Take My Heart." Bob Fine, an engineer, had opened a studio in upstate New York at Stoney Point. It was built into a mountain and was a natural echo chamber. It was never really used for a pop record. I drove Barelli's master tapes up there and we re-recorded them through that natural echo chamber. Those tapes were of "Here in My Heart," featuring Al Martino. The record became a smash hit because of that echo sound that made it even better. Our song was the next release, and it was a so-so hit. I ran into Al Martino at the Friars Club in Los Angeles one night and told him that story. He had never known that I was involved with the re-recording of that song with the natural echo effect.

Fred Waring had a radio show and later a television show. He used to see all the songpluggers at the Horn & Hardart Automat at 46th Street and Broadway, New York. They had a little balcony, and we met there. All the songpluggers came, and it was a big plug to get. My friend, Patsy Garrett, was one of the singers on the show.

In 1952, Joy Music picked up a Broadway show called *New Faces Of 1952*, which had a good score and featured top-rate artists, mainly unknowns, but many of them soon went on to become well-known. They included Ronnie Graham, Eartha Kitt, Alice Ghostly, Paul Lynde, Carol Lawrence, Robert Clary, June Carroll, and writer Melvin Brooks. The show featured songs such as "Guess Who I Saw Today," "Love Is a Simple Thing," and "Monotonus," a show-stopping finale featuring Earth Kitt. We did well with the score and the show played to sold out crowds. Because of her popularity, Eartha recorded "Santa Baby," which was written for us by Phil Springer. That song was a big hit and soon became a standard. Melvin Brooks later became known as Mel Brooks. Some years later, I went over to the office of Thomas Golubic, who is the music consultant for the *Six Feet Under* television show. He pulled out a CD of an artist and said how talented he was. The CD featured Ronnie Graham. Thomas was surprised when I told him that I had worked with Ronnie way back 1952.

Guy Mitchell was going with Jackie Loughery, Miss USA 1952, the first Miss USA. He met her in Hollywood while he was doing a television show, and they were later married. One night while he was doing a show at The Enchanted Room in Yonkers, I was there with Paul Insetta and his wife. Paul was Guy's road manager. Paul and I went to the back to check the sound in the room. The house band was on stage with their singer, Jerry Vale. I listened, and then I mentioned to Paul that he sounded different and had a great voice. Paul took it from there and invited him down to his apartment. Guy was staying there most of the time and he was always playing guitar and singing. One night, Jerry Vale called and came down. Everyone hit it off well. They all sang, and Paul took him under his wing. I was not into management yet and just stayed in publishing. Paul was close to Mitch Miller through Guy, was able to get Jerry a contract at Columbia Records. The rest is history, except that Paul left Guy and handled Jerry from then on. I have always felt that if it was not for me, Jerry would still be in The Bronx, where he lived. Jerry was in the right place at the right time.

By 1953, the time came for me to get a new car again, and I bought a 1953 Olds Delta 88 convertible, a snazzy car. It was great. The price was $3,300.

9

Why Does a Woman Cry?

Bob Merrill wrote "How Much Is That Doggie in the Window?" a song we thought was so cute that I gave it to Patti Page and Jack Rael, never really knowing what would happen. She recorded it, and it became one of the biggest hit records ever. Jack, by-the-way, did the little bark that you hear on that record, a fact that is seldom mentioned. Over the years, they recorded more songs for me, and those songs did quite well.

Patty was known as "The Singing Rage," and when Jack and Patti bought their boat, they named it the *Rage*. Patti was a huge success at that time, with one hit after another, but "How Much Is That Doggie in the Window?" was such a monster hit that George Joy gave me a summer bonus. When I came back from one road trip, he once yelled at me for not putting in enough dollars on my expense account. He said that I should go over it because he was sure I had left something out. He really liked me.

Bob Merrill was an excellent writer of both words and music. However, he could not read a note of music, nor could he play any instrument. He kept melodies entirely in his head. He had a toy xylophone and played the melodies on it. There was a piano player in the Brill Building who had an office, and he transcribed the music into notes on paper as Bob played the tunes on his toy.

When Patti Page and Guy Mitchell were booked into the Mastbaum Theater in Philadelphia for a week, I went down there to escort him around the various radio stations. He was with his road manager, Paul Insetta, and we decided to order a late snack in the room after the show. Guy called room service for a steak and some garlic bread, but he was told that the kitchen was closed. They said they would work something up for us, and in no time, up came steaks, bread, and garlic cloves. Guy ate all the garlic, and the next day, he stunk so terribly that we couldn't stand to get anywhere near him. We bought everything possible to reduce the odor, including every type of mouth freshener. Patti hated garlic and just couldn't stand his smell, but their show included a closing duet that featured the two of them singing "We're Glad To Do This Show" or a song like that while linked together arm in arm. Because of Guy's horrific smell, she made a last minute change to their routine that night and sang the song from the far side of the stage.

Jack was going to cruise on the *Rage* up to Newburyport, Massachusetts, where Patti was appearing nearby in a club. He asked me if I would join him for the trip. I talked to George and he said that I should go ahead. We started out with Jack's captain at the helm, but I soon took the wheel a few times and enjoyed it. The *Rage* was a Chris Craft thirty-four-foot Double Cabin Flying Bridge. We got to Cuttyhunk, an island in Long Island Sound off the Cape Cod Canal. The Coast Guard came while we were having dinner in a restaurant and ordered everyone to leave, dash for the Canal, and tie up at Sandwich, an inlet at the other end of the canal. It seemed that Hurricane Carol was bearing down on the shore. That journey was my first long trip, and I was put out over the prospect of being storm-tossed again. We left port and made it as far as Sandwich. That night, all the fishing boats came in and tied up together. Compared to them, we were a peewee. Before long, the hurricane hit, and with the winds came rain that swamped over the deck and into the cabin. The Captain and I were up all night for fear of what might happen next. Jack slept through the maelstrom as if we were adrift in seas as calm as glass. We managed to weather the storm, and soon were on our way the next day as if nothing had happened.

Sherm Feller and his wife, Judy (Valentine), who was also a singer, were at the club where Patti was singing. Sherm was going down to do his all night show, and he asked me to go with him. As we were driving from town, he made a wrong u-turn, and we were immediately pulled over by a cop. The cop comes to the window and explained to Sherm what he did.

"What would you do?" Sherm objected. "I have a hysterical wife yelling I went the wrong way, the guy in the back yelling I should have taken the right, and so forth!"

The cop just laughed, and then he let us go. Sherm was a good comedian, too, and this event gave him a great story to retell many times. Sherm also went on to be the announcer at Wonderland, the dog track, and he was also the announcer at Fenway Park for the Red Sox until he passed away.

By coincidence, Lucky Carle was once in Boston at the same time as me. Sherm talked us into going to the dog races. The beginning went well; we pooled $20 each and made one bet on each race, not knowing much about dog races. We came out ahead, but then decided to put the winnings on one dog in the last race. Of course, we had taken out our $20. We both came up with the name together because it had something to do with music. We bet it. The race started, and then to everyone's shock, the dog stopped to piss, and then he stopped to crap. We laughed so hard!

Bernie Wayne, the songwriter I wrote about earlier, had an office in the Brill Building where Joy Music was on the fifth floor. We songpluggers used to go from one office to another and just shoot the breeze. It was an open business and we all congratulated someone if they had a hit song, which was great in those days. There were always a group of guys talking in front of the building. We had two great restaurants inside the building, Jack Dempsey's on one side, and The Turf on the other side. Jack Amiel owned both of them, and we ate at both of them. Dempsey was there everyday and sat at a table near the window right by the front door. He shook everyone's hand and posed for pictures with his fans, which were great thrills for some people.

I once walked out the front door and ran into a friend that had a small record out, but in those days, some time usually passed before anyone made money. Steve Lawrence was always looking for a good song to sing and record. One day, we were talking and he borrowed a dime for a cup of coffee, (which he never paid back). I used to give him songs when he was on *The Tonight Show* with Steve Allen and, of course, Edie Gorme.

As I said, Bernie Wayne had an office in the Brill Building, and he used to rehearse singers there, as well as coach all the singers for the Miss America contest shows. He always had parties and it was a good place to hang out. I used to spend many weekends at the Concord, a hotel in the Catskills. Bernie used to go with me, and we shared a room. It was a great place to go.

Grossingers had the same group, always with good talent, especially the comedians. One weekend we were at The Grossinger at the same time the Monticello Race Track was opening, and Paul Grossinger had something to do with it. I believe he was on the Board of Directors. He invited us that night and we sat in his box.

The morning show at WNEW had a lot of changes, but the nucleus was always there. Gene Raeburn and Jack Lescoulie both went on to other stations and major shows. Gene's brother, Jim Robessa, wrote "What Good Is Somebody New?" With my help, he was able to give the song to Richard Hayman, who was the A&R man at Mercury Records. Hayman liked the song and gave singer Bobby Wayne a chance to record it. Hayman thought it could be a hit, so Jim Robessa, asked me to publish it for him. Al and I had thought about going into business, but until that time, we didn't have the right thing.

Being totally honest to George Joy, I told him, "I don't think it would be fair to you if I stayed while doing other work on the side."

He then said to me, "You can't leave until you find someone to take your place."

I noticed a little tear in his eye. That guy liked me so much that once in 1954 I had an accident with my 88 convertible and it was laid up for a few days. He gave me his new Cadillac to use and had Eddie drive him home. A few days later, I was walking along Broadway and I ran into Harvey Geller, who was the promo man at the Distributor for London Records. I asked him if he was looking for a job. He was, and I took him up to Joy and he got the job. He stayed there a long time before moving on to *Billboard Magazine*. Then, I was able to leave, and we parted friends with Joy wishing me luck.

Al was playing organ for *Young Widder Brown*, which was a daily soap opera. The shows at Hummert Radio Features where he worked went off the air as television was starting to grow. Frank Hummert gave him that show. At the same time, Al was doing all the arrangements for the Ben Yost singers. Yost had four or five different singing groups performing at a lot of shows for conventions. They had an office in 1650 Broadway, and Ben was closing that office. Al told him that we would take it over and keep it open because the groups were still working and they needed a place. It was only two rooms, but exactly what we needed. That enterprise was a big undertaking for us, but we thought positive. The record came out. I took my trips and got it played, but I guess we were wrong. It was not that good a song. We got played all over, but it just didn't make it.

Our income largely came from Broadcast Music, Inc. (BMI) and the American Society of Composers, Authors, and Publishers (ASCAP), both of which were collection agencies that collected money from radio and TV for performances of songs, and then paid with four disbursements throughout each year. There we were with an office and two publishing houses, Kohn Music, which was associated with ASCAP, but was later to be called Creston Music, and Alroy Music, which was associated with BMI.

We had become so well-known that people started coming off the street to play us their new songs. One day, Bob Jackenthal and Adam Kniest came in unexpectedly. Bob was a singer and Adam was his piano player. They played us their material, and we liked it so much that we decided to do a recording session. Bob had a great voice with a unique sound, and we picked four of his songs that we thought he could do well: Awful Weary," "Ali Baba," "Tomorrow is Another Day," and "Why Does a Woman Cry?" Al did the arrangements and came up with great orchestrations. Those were our first major recording sessions, and we spent a lot of time on them so the recordings would turn out well. We decided on "Why Does a Woman Cry?" as the push side, and backed it up with "Ali Baba." We changed Bob's name to Bob Jaxon, and then we put the record out to see what would be the public's response.

Barclay Records was born when we bought the rights from the manager of Bob Manning, a singer whose recordings were released on Capitol Records. They just used the label to record Manning's songs, and the time came when they were no longer using the name. That made it easier for us rather than going through all the troublesome paperwork to start one up from scratch with an entirely new name.

In 1955, old-fashioned twelve-inch 78 rpm records were still being produced, but the new, Hi-Fidelity five-inch 45 rpm records were just starting to come out on the market. Radio stations needed to have songs on both formats until newer equipment was installed, so we had to press newly released records in both formats, and we did.

I used New England as the jump off area, especially Boston. I made up packages, labeled them, and made sure everyone got them on the same day. There were some feuding DJs who wouldn't play a record if someone else got it first. Nevertheless, I got them all out in the mail on a Friday so that they all received them on the following Monday.

Dottie Checchi, the librarian at WHDH, which was the top radio station in Boston, fell in love with "Why Does A Woman Cry". She cried when she heard it. She also liked Bob's voice, which was a perfect combination. She started programming the record for frequent plays on their station, and soon it became Pick of the Week. Bob Clayton played it, and I like to believe that all the guys did it for me up there.

Another Station, WORL, was picking up listeners because it was run by my friend, Norm Prescott. Another friend, Stan Richards, had a top show on the station. Stan also did a Saturday afternoon television show that was broadcast from The Totem Pole, a very well-known dance hall outside of Boston. It was a big show and Howard Johnson was the sponsor. Stan called and wanted Bob Jaxon for that show. I was walking on air because Al and I had our own publishing company with a hit song, we have a record company with a hit record, and I had an artist in Bob Jaxon with a possible hit song, a possible hit record, and two other recordings waiting to be released, one of which we expected would be a hit.

In 1955, Rock and Roll began to gain in popularity, but there was still room for a good ballad. We were on the ground floor in that era, which also was a time during when small publishers, record companies, and writer/artists were getting their starts.

In those days there were places called "one stops." They supplied records for juke boxes and also some record shops around the area. One was run by a guy named Jerry Flatto. He also was a good friend and I used to stay at his house once in a while. He found out that "Why Does a Woman Cry?" was mine. He called and needed records right away for sale. The record was being played like the national anthem. I couldn't believe that the song was a hit.

Bob, Al, and I got into the car and started out for Boston. We made a few stops along the way and told the stations in Hartford and New Haven what was happening. I couldn't hit any more stations because we were booked on the television show with Stan on Saturday and we were running out of time.

We grabbed all the records we had. We only pressed 1,000 45rpm records and 1,000 78rpm records. We placed a new order with RCA for another thousand 45 rpm records and 1,000 78 rpm records. We really didn't have much money left, but we had to do it. Bob did the television show with Stan. Bob was a pretty good-looking guy, but he was still green as far as being an entertainer. Lip-synching to a record is not easy, but since he wrote the song, that made it a little easier for him. He did a good job, and Stan was impressed and thanked us for being there so soon and making the show. Bob was well-received.

Stan had a teenage audience, and all the bandstand dance shows were for teenagers. I looked around the crowd and they loved the record. We could always tell if they were quiet or something like that, and Bob was winning the audience. To be in town just when all the stations were playing his record was important. Everything was going well. It was a great feeling when we were in the car and twisting the radio dial to hear the record all over the air.

We returned to New York, where Norm Prescott was on WNEW. He went on the air with the record and was the first to play it in New York. I'm sure he liked the record. He made a big thing about playing it first in New York. He was a good friend, and I am also sure he was happy for us.

That Monday, I made the rounds to all the stations in New York and shipped some records to Philadelphia. The reception was good, but not like Boston. We were getting plays in New York and the song was added to

Why Does a Woman Cry? 43

most of the play lists. Sam Clark called me from Boston. He was with Cadence Records and Archie Bleyer. He confirmed that "Why Does a Woman Cry?" was a hit. He asked what I was going to do and said that I would need a lot of money to get it started. He said he would put the record out on Cadence Records for us with a good deal. Cadence had just had a hit with "Davy Crockett" by Bill Hayes, as well as Archie Bleyer's "Hernando's Hideaway," and he was in a good position to have another hit then.

We could have done many things differently. Second guessing never worked, so we decided to give them the record. We got all our money back, but here's what happened: the lull between the playing and the release on Cadence Records hurt.

In two weeks, Sam Clark left Cadence Records and went to work as the President of AMPAR Records (Paramount Pictures label, ABC Records). Archie really didn't want the record because he didn't produce it, and Al's name was on the label as conductor, which was a minor overall, but a major point to Archie. They never worked the record. Sam Clark screwed us. I don't think they put anything behind the record and just sold the orders that were there from the work we did.

It didn't go any further than Boston, Philadelphia, and New York. They sold 25,000 records. That was the first time I have ever heard about labels taking a record to kill it, and that's exactly what happened.

Meanwhile, we got a call from a club out on Long Island called the San Souci. They wanted Bob for the weekend. We had the arrangements made with a good arranger (Al), who worked cheap. We put something together and we accepted a paying job for Bob. I guess the record was getting enough play in New York. We did the show. The opening act was Pat Cooper, a young comedian. The club looked nicely crowded, and I guess they did good business for the weekend with Bob. All went well.

Lonnie Starr, another DJ who I was close to at WNEW, was playing the record and he asked for the favor of having Bob sing at his Rotary Club meeting in Valley Stream, Long Island. Connie Frances was also to be there, so we accepted, of course. Al was prepared to play for Bob, but he didn't know that he also had to play for Connie. She had that record, "Who's Sorry Now?" It had that bouncing piano Rock and Roll sound. Al did so well with her live rendition on stage that she later said no other piano player played it as good as him. Those few weeks were exciting; I must say that we were on a high. No matter what happened, we went on and kept it going after that. We tried everything, and we kept the momentum going for awhile.

"Why Does a Woman Cry?" was a success as a song, aside from Bob's recording. With the action we had, we got a couple of cover records made by other artists such as Kitty White on Mercury Records and one with Michael Strange on RKO Records.

10

Limehouse Blues

1955 was probably the documented beginning of Rock and Roll music, and it was also the beginning for writers and recording groups like The Platters and The Four Lads, but Bill Haley and the Comets started it. The Rock and Roll era also began the emergence of small labels and small publishers. We were in on it, but at the time, we were just on the fringe.

People came through our office with material. We were located at 1650 Broadway (actually the entrance was on 51st Street). It should have been called Brill Building North, or something like that. It was full of publishers, all small except for the one on the second floor, Irving Berlin. Also in the building were a lot of small but growing record companies.

After Ben Yost closed his office and moved operations to California, we took it over, but of course Al was still going to run the singers for Ben. He still had groups of all sizes and big voices. They were known as The Vikings, The Varsity Eight, six voices, eight voices, any size anyone wanted. Al wrote all the arrangements over the years. It worked out pretty good for us.

I knew all the singers. One was Brian Davies. He was a pretty good baritone, but also had a fine voice for pop music. He auditioned and was accepted as one of the singers. He also went on to do Arthur Godfrey's talent show. He went on as a regular on the morning Godfrey show on CBS radio. At the time, the show had The McGuire Sisters, Anita Bryant, a Miss America contestant, Myoshi Umeki, Archie Bleyer, The Cordettes, and some others that were on and off at different times. I contacted the show with music and used to take Anita, Myoshi and Brian out for breakfast across the street at a coffee shop in the CBS Building.

The Ben Yost Vikings used to play a lot of club dates for an agent named Charlie Peterson. I went along just to see what was happening, as I had to keep active. At one of the dates, there was a large group, some kind of convention where I saw an outstanding act featuring Phil Ramone, a left-handed violin player. I did nothing, and we just became friends. Later, he became one of the top record producers.

At one of the shows, I met Jack Ladelle, a guy who sang and played thirty-two instruments. He had them all with him, and he performed an amazing, fast-moving act. I asked him to come and see me at the office. I didn't know what I wanted. I did not have a contract with Bob Jaxon, but I was a publisher and a record company President, even though I was not worth 5¢ as a President at that time. My friendship and knowledge of the business were my fortes. Jack came to see us and we talked. With a handshake, he agreed to see what I could do for him, but I did say we would be his publisher because he had some songs he wrote.

I was close with a lot of the heads of various radio stations, and of course they wanted to do good for their station. WNEW had a daily variety show at noon. I approached Steve White, who was with WNBC at that time in the program department. I told him I had come across a talent who played thirty-two instruments and sang like Bing Crosby. (Jack did have that kind of voice). He was sold. I always considered myself a good songplugger, and a good songplugger could sell anything. If a guy can sell a piece of paper with notes on it to someone, he could sell anything.

Steve set up a meeting with Jack. He then said that we should have him do a one-hour audition just like we would do the show. He decided to use NBC studio musicians, and he booked a studio. We worked on the script and put together what we would do built around Jack's arrangements and the instruments he played, trying to put as much of those in as we could. Steve gave us a quartet from the NBC staff, but not just any quartet, they were Johnny Guarnieri on piano, Eddie Safranski on Bass, Mundell Lowe on guitar, and Don Lamond on drums. If you were putting a group together and given these guys, you would have thought that you had died and gone to heaven, and your life would have been complete. They were the best.

We did the audition, and it turned out great. The band was top rate. We gave them solos just like a real show. Jack played his instruments and sang, and we were recording all of it, of course. Steve played it for the powers that be, and they liked it, so we were in, even though I still had no contract with Jack. However, it was Al's job to handle the arrangements if any were needed, and my job to play the records. There were four records to be played on every show, and I picked them. Al picked the live music and all Jack had to do was show up, sing, and play. It went well. Al and I saw all the songpluggers, and that felt good to be on the other side for a change. We were good to everyone and we were well-liked by all. We did a good job. The show was doing fine. I was dealing with Steve and others as any manager would do.

My secret was that I knew Jack could only play a few songs on each instrument, and he could only play the guitar extremely well. He faked the others, such as the saxophone, trumpet, and piano. When he played piano, he added runs up down the keys, which were impressive and helped create the illusion that he was an outstanding pianist, when in reality he was just a talented faker. I made sure that no one knew the truth.

I was contacting record companies. A friend of mine, Gene Becker, was an A&R man at Columbia Records. I went to see him and told him what I had. He was interested after I told him he could play the whole record by himself, something that Les Paul and Mary Ford were also doing. I asked him if he would come to NBC to see the show. He came to the studio one day and liked what he saw and heard. The session would be inexpensive; the only cost was for the studio time.

In the space of six weeks, I got Jack a radio show broadcasting for one hour five times a week, and a record contract with the biggest and hottest record company at the time. The session was booked. Gene told me to do anything we wanted. We picked two songs: "Limehouse Blues," a well-known standard that I thought would be good for Jack because he was doing it in his act and could play the tune on all the instruments. The second side was "Forever," a song he wrote that we used as the show's theme song, and one that he could sing well.

All was set. We went to one of Columbia's recording studios, the old Liederkranz Hall, a studio big enough to handle the New York Philharmonic when they recorded. We started recording the basic guitar track, and then we went from one tape machine to another, each time layering on another track. Les Paul had also become known for his multi-track recordings, but his were made with his own machine that he had personally built with a few tracks on it. When tracks were overdubbed, each remained as clear as the next. On our makeshift multi-track recording set-up, we kept losing the high notes because the more times we went from tape machine to tape machine, the first few tracks became progressively weaker. We had to do some of them over. The effort was trial and error and took some time, but we finally got it done with Jack playing all the instruments he could, and singing "Forever," as well as accompanying himself for the other side.

Believe it or not, the end results were quite good. The completed product had a nice sound for just one person playing all the instruments. Most importantly, those at Columbia liked it. The record got released in a rush because of the radio show. I couldn't believe how fast all this was going.

I went out on the road to get it played. The record failed to go over. No one seemed interested, and I had to conclude that it didn't matter that the artist played all the instruments because just listening to the record, no one knew that fact. There was no accompanying video, so the end result was unimpressive. "Limehouse Blues" had a good sound, but for that time, the song just wasn't strong enough. We got radio play, but the record just didn't sell.

We moved into the second thirteen-week series at NBC. Jack was starting to handle his own future at the station, and he was dictating what he wanted. Steve called me to get him off his back. Jack thought he was great, as often happens to most stars, but as good as they are with their talent, they can't manage business, and they seldom learn to leave business to their manager or agent, with whom they'd be better off. Jack thought he could do everything by himself, so he dropped Al and me, and then by rubbing people at the station the wrong way, he got cancelled.

Gene Becker called and wanted to do another session with Jack. I said I didn't handle him any longer and told him what happened. Gene told me he just wanted to try again for me. He said he could do without Jack.

After being dropped by Columbia and having his show cancelled, Jack surprised me by calling back. "What do we do now?" he asked.

Goodbye, Jack Ladelle. We did a good selling job at the right time, but I had never drawn up a contract with any of my artists. I was a publisher and that's what I did best. The experience was a lesson for me to always put an agreement on paper.

Al and I only took $75 a week each from Jack's check, but we did all the programming work, and Al did all the arrangements without taking one extra cent. They were paying Jack scale, but five days a week was pretty good. He was doing fine money wise. It was good experience for us.

People continued to unexpectedly come in off the street and work the building. One day, in came Neal Sedaka, a piano-playing singer, with his mother. We saw him, and he started playing his songs for us. Al and I were on our last buck. He sounded pretty good, but he also wanted to be an artist. We were not ready at that time, so unfortunately, we passed on him.

Other people came through and wanted us to produce recording sessions for them, and they were willing to pay for the sessions, but our deal was to be the publisher of their songs. We were also picking up songs and

Limehouse Blues 49

Guty Mitchell

Renee & Bob Jaxon, Gene Bock & Shirley

Roy & Jack Rael

Brian Davies

Mort Fleishmann

pushing them.

While Al was still appearing on *Young Widder Brown,* Sean Downey, a songwriter, stopped in one day and left a song for us. His other name was Morton Downey, Jr. He dropped some other songs off a few days later, and he did have a couple of good ones.

We started to produce some recording sessions. We had been picking up songs, and the songwriters advised us that we could publish them if we could get them recorded. Some were good. Some guy who owned a trucking company came through and he had a niece who was a singer. The artist's name was Edith Lanza (no relation to Mario). He wanted to record her. We told him we would, but we could not promise anything other than giving the session a good try, as well as sending the recording to disc jockeys and working it. They accepted the terms, and then we set it up.

Al did the arrangements, and we recorded Edith Lanza singing four songs all in one session. In those days, recording sessions were live, and because it was her first session, Edith was a little nervous. She sang Downey's "In the Chapel on the Hill," and she did a good job. The other side was a song with an exciting gypsy melody and a solid arrangement. She sang with a large orchestra, because the type of songs she sang needed strings and other instruments of that kind, a high-class session. The orchestra sounded sensational and helped make the session top rate. We took nothing for it because we were hoping for a hit. We released it, but nothing happened.

A few years earlier, I joined The Friar's Club in New York. Others were inducted on the same night, including Paul Cohen, one of the top Country and Western A&R men, and Tommy Leonetti, a well-know singer. Lunch at The Friar's Club was a ball. It was the only place around town to go when you were alone, and a member got to sit with Henny Youngman, Jack E. Leonard, Milton Berle, and many others who happened to be in town.

The Luncheon Roasts at the Friar's Club are still talked about today. I used to take Al before he also joined the club, and DJ's like Lonnie Starr, and others. The roasts were held at The Copacabana and they always sold out. The list of people in the audience read like a Who's Who of the entertainment business. The dais featured every top comedian in their prime, and the roasts were great just for mingling.

I was single then and could spend much time at radio stations. Sitting in the studio with Martin Block at WNEW in the 1940s and 1950s was a ball. He had many stories. In fact, I was once invited to his Penthouse apartment one New Years Eve. Of course, the invitation came through his son, Gene, but I was that close to Martin, also. Gene was married to a pretty gal named Shirley. They lived in Fort Lee, New Jersey, and I was out to his place quite often. I got my records played, of course, but they were my friends. Most of my friends were in the business. Gene programmed Martin's show.

Martin Block owned a Bentley. He had been driving on the New Jersey Turnpike and had a flat tire. He called the local Bentley dealership. They came out and changed all four tires for free. Another time when he was on the Turnpike, he was driving along and was stopped by a State Trooper for speeding. I'm not sure, but I think the speed limit was 50 mph. The cop said he was doing seven miles over the limit. He asked the cop when his speedometer was last checked. The cop had no answer. Martin then told him that there was a 10 percent discrepancy in the accuracy between any two speedometers, and he said that if and when they went to court, he would embarrass the Trooper. No ticket was issued.

Martin was a gadget man and had a wire recorder, a predecessor of the tape recorder. He was the most interesting man, and he was actually the first DJ in New York. I remember listening to his *Make Believe Ballroom* on the radio when I was a kid.

While at WNEW in New York, I was sitting in a studio and Bob Landers was on the air. I had met him at another station when I was on a trip to Baltimore. He was doing a live commercial and he turned to me with this jar in his hand and said, "You know, with a name like Smuckers, it has to be good." That was the first time I heard that statement. Either he made it up then and there on the spot, or it was written in the script, but to this day Bob, is still doing Smucker commercials. His voice still sounds the same, so when you hear that spot, it's Bob.

11

Two Little Angels

1955 was a busy year for Al and me. We released many records on Barclay, but we still did not have a hit, except for "Why Does a Woman Cry?" by Bob Jaxon. Bob and I used to have coffee and cake in a coffee shop at 1650 Broadway called the B&G. On Wednesday matinee days, a young singer named Barbra Streisand always came in, and Bob always talked to anyone. He and Barbra always talked, and he learned that she was in *Fanny*, the show next door, working as the understudy for the lead.

I liked opera, and there was a melody at the end of *Rigoletto* by Verdi that I thought would make a good song. Bob wrote a lyric to the melody, and we had a song called "To Belong." I told Bob that I approved him showing it around. Teddy Powell, a friend of ours, had a publishing house and had heard that Don Rondo was looking for a song. He played "To Belong" for Don and he liked it. He was on Jubilee Records, a major label then. We let Teddy have the song. The session was set. Don came in with pneumonia and proceeded with the session, but the result was another flop for me because he just sang words without any feeling. Teddy secured another record of "To Belong" with a singer named Jimmy Breedlove on Epic.

We didn't give up. We met a couple of guys on a club date who wanted to record. They had a cute idea, a song called "Rock and Roll Yodel." It was good to be different; you never know. We used Johnny Guarnieri and a group. Les Vegas and Billy Woods, the name alone warranted a play, but the song didn't make it. I got the play, but as we used to say, "It isn't in the groove."

We then released the other two sides of Edith Lanza, strictly for the backer. However, one of the sides, "Two Little Angels," was written by Bob Jaxon. I sent it out to my stations, but nothing could help it.

About the same time as the Jack Ladelle show, NBC was airing a big band show called *Bandstand*. Johnny Guarnieri was the piano player on it and he was given a solo spot. We became quite friendly with Johnny, and when we were talking one day, he said he had all these songs, and wanted us to do something with them, and also wanted us to put him in ASCAP. We published his material and also printed the sheet music because they were strictly piano pieces and we knew that we could sell copies. Also, we were not sure what payments we would receive for his solo performance on *Bandstand* (if there would be any),in the ASCAP quarterly statement , which would come out in nine months. We didn't even think of it then.

After we used Johnny for the Les Vegas session, we decided to record him with his own group that was actually made up of men from the NBC shows: Jack Lesberg on bass, Bunny Shawker on drums, and George Barnes on guitar. We did four songs. One of them, "A Gliss To Remember," did get a lot of play when I took it around, but I guess it was the wrong time. All four sides were good, including "Pipsqueak Parade," "Top Of The Piano," and "Wibbly Wobbly Walrus," which was the backside of "A Gliss To Remember" and had a great solo by George Barnes, as well as some great solo bass playing by Jack Lesberg. It was a so-called turntable hit, which meant that it got played but didn't sell.

We knew that we had to get with the times. Rock and Roll was big, and recording all that pop stuff didn't bring success. However, we did go in and do a few more with Johnny and his group, enough for a complete LP. We never were able to release it.

Bobby Bernard, a manager, was a friend of Al, and Bobby had Jeanne Geary, a girl singer with a big voice that he wanted to record. We heard her, and we came up with the idea of doing music more close to what was happening in 1956. Rock and Roll was gaining in popularity, so we had befriended a Black tenor sax player, (Buddy Lucas), who had his own group and was performing on a lot of sessions. We met him as he was a songwriter and had shown us some material. We got together with him and Jeanne and picked some songs that he wrote. "Mama's Tired" had the 1950s Rock and Roll pounding beat, and our recording featured a great tenor sax solo by Buddy. Buddy's band was great. Jeanne sang it full, robust, and solid. We released it in a couple of weeks, and then off we went to Cleveland, the top record town in the country, with Allan Freed and Bill Randall among others. They listed in all the trade papers and what they played went to the top. In that year, payola was in its glory. I never paid for a play; I never had to. I romanced the DJs with lunch and dinner, and that was it, but I was in the middle of all that payola that was going on. So, I didn't get the record played much. The play I did get was not saturated, so that was that.

However, that trip to Cleveland was not a total loss. I stopped at a radio station and met a guy that was to become my closest friend and brother-in-law. Mort Fleischmann, who was the producer of a morning show featuring Johnny Andrews. A few years before, he was producing the Kathy Norris show at NBC in New York. From then on, we became close friends because they moved the Johnny Andrews show to New York at NBC and we spent a lot of time together.

Al and I wouldn't quit, even though our money was running out. We had to give it another shot. We looked for material to record The Vikings, a Ben Yost group, and Bob Jaxon again. We went in and did a session, two sides with The Vikings and two sides with Bob. Needless to say, all the sides came out okay in our eyes and ears, so we released them.

I went on the road to get the records played, but no success. Payola was killing us, and the Top 40 play lists were becoming tighter. I tried everything. It really was getting me down. I knew we had given it a good shot, but by 1956, we decided to call it quits. Because of the play we did get for Bob Jaxon, he was able to land himself on RCA Victor. He came to me first and asked me what to do, and I told him he was on his own. We had no paper between us. We always stayed close, and he went on to record for them, scoring some turntable hits, but that was all.

I was ready to do something: I found out that Dave Kapp, who opened his own record company, Kapp Records, was looking for a promotion man. I met with him, and learned that the opportunity was part-time, which was perfect for me. He had just released "Autumn Leaves" with Roger Williams, and he was about to release some new stuff.

There was a Jane Morgan record, "Fascination," that he wanted played. The song went on to become a hit for him. I remember I had to pick Jane up at a photo studio in the Village. It was a magazine shoot for a Sunday newspaper. I got there and announced to the receptionist that I was there to pick her up. We were going to one of the radio stations for an interview. A few days later, the following item appeared in Walter Winchell's column: "Jane Morgan's dating a local named Roy Cohn. He anti Roy Cohn (sic)." I only stayed at Kapp Records for a few months. Dave had his son, Mickey, coming out of school, and he wanted me to take him around and show him the ropes. Mickey went on to become a Vice President at Warner Bros. Records and Special Products. We have always remained friends.

I was never out of work. As soon as the Kapp Record job ended, I was called by Bob Merrill, the writer of "How Much is That Doggie in the Widow?" and the other songs at Joy Music. He had started his own management and publishing company. He offered me the promo job. They had a record coming out with The Baker Sisters on RCA Records. Also, as a partner with Bob was Murray Kaufman, who later became known as "Murray the K," one of the top DJs in the New York market and in syndication. Murray and I went on the road with The Baker Sisters, to work the record starting in Boston and ending in Cleveland. The power of RCA and two pretty girls got us into all the radio stations, and we got our initial plays. However, when we left town, the song kept making only the bottom of every list, and it went no further.

There were a few more releases Bob had coming out, but nothing that meant anything. He then started to close his office and just write.

All Al and I needed was one good hit, and then we would have been all set. In 1955, Al and Edna opened the Barclay Record Shop where they lived in Forest Hills. They were doing okay, and I helped some evenings and on Saturdays. We got lots of help from the distributors we knew quite well. Many carried us on consignment and others got us hard-to-get records, such as Elvis Presley, RCA, and other artists when other shops couldn't get them. The store was also selling the VM Tape machine and Dictograph HI-FI record player.

Out of nowhere, I got a call from Fred Alhert, Jr., a songplugger and the son of the great songwriter, Fred Alhert. He was leaving Leo Feist Music, one of the top publishers, and he asked if he could recommend me for the job. Of course, I said yes. I met with the professional Manager, Norman Foley, and we hit it off. He said I'd have to meet with Mickey Scopp, the General Manager (the same Mickey Scopp who was Al's boss at Hummert Air Features). After a short meeting, I was then with Leo Feist Music, part of The Big Three.

The Big Three were major music publishers who represented major film companies: Robbins Music, affiliated with MGM, which was, at the time, probably the largest film company; Leo Feist Music was the publisher for 20th Century Fox Film Corporation; and Miller Music was independent and the smaller of the three firms. Teddy Black, who at one time had a big band and had since moved into music publishing, was with Miller Music. He and I seemed to hit it off, and we traveled together whenever we could.

Mort Fleischmann had since moved back to New York. NBC moved Johnny Andrews to New York and gave him a show, the same type he was doing in Cleveland. Mort was still with him. The show was soon cancelled, and Mort got a great opportunity to move into promotions with Al Rylander at NBC Network. They worked with personalities on NBC and did the promo for them and the shows, a big job for Mort. We remained close and became mostly social and not business friendly.

Al and I finally got some good news with our publishing companies. Even though inactivated, they are always making money. We finally got an ASCAP statement for performances, but they were usually nine months behind. We had been getting quarterly statements for Kohn Music, but never much on it. All of a sudden, a statement came in for the second quarter of 1957, and it showed that we had earned $16,000 for the work we did getting air play with our records and the Johnny Guarnieri material. It finally paid off! Back in 1957, $16,000 was big money. If it had come sooner, or even if we knew it would have been that big, we might have kept going.

Those checks came for another few quarters, not as big, but sizable. After the fact, our work had proven to be a profitable venture for is. We kept the companies, but Kohn Music became known as Creston Music Company, named after our school, of course.

In the late 50s and early 60s there was an important dance show on TV hosted by Mrs. Arthur Murray. Arthur Murray opened the show and never smiled. A song was written called "Arthur, You Should Smile More" and Ray Carter, the orchestra conductor on the show, recorded it wirh The Arthur Murray Orchestra on RCA records. Our Creston Music was the publisher. We also had two John Guarnieri songs called "Whistle Stop" and "Movin Along" recorded by The Glenn Miller Orchestra conducted by Ray McKinnley on RCA rceords.

12

Volare

In 1957, I was still living with my parents, and I was thirty-three years old. In those days, apartments were hard to come by and there was no reason for me to have one. I wasn't making much money while I was in business. In fact, most of my money was going out for the businesses. I was living on $1 a day.

I decided the time had come for me to move out on my own. One member of The Vikings was moving to California and he had an apartment off Central Park West, 18 West 70th Street. He was leaving the furniture and everything. We struck a deal, and I had it for $130 a month, which wasn't bad for a living room, small kitchen, and separate bedroom. When I told my mom, she didn't take it too well. She never wanted me to leave, but the deal was done. That apartment today would rent for $3,000 a month or more.

Al and Edna were still with the record shop. They carried some good hi-fi items and tape machines. When I moved into the apartment, I bought a tape machine and a Dictograph hi-fi from their store. I had a lot of pre-recorded tapes and records, such as "The 1812 Overture" that featured canons. In those days, I also started taping The Metropolitan Opera on Saturday radio broadcasts. For years, I kept fifty or sixty operas on tape with the debuts of artists such as Franco Corelli and Joan Sutherland, and a tape from 1959 of *Faust*, sung by Jussi Bjoerling playing Faust. I played those tapes so loud the walls would move. Some of the neighbors liked it, and no one ever complained. They had thick walls in those old buildings.

Two of my neighbors were Bill Lewis, a tenor with The Metropolitan Opera, and Earl Wild, who went on to become a well-known pianist. They lived on the sixth floor and I was on the seventh floor, and we used to meet in the elevator and talked music. One day, I mentioned that I had a certain pre-recorded tape of "La Boutique Fantasque." Earl told me that a certain ballet dancer was coming in from Russia and had the rights to perform it first here in the United States. A few weeks later, I got a call from him saying that the dancer was in his apartment. He asked if they could come up and hear "La Boutique Fantasque," among other things. Up came Bill, Earl, and the dancer in kimonos. I wasn't into the gay culture, but I've been around those who were, and I never was hit upon, but I got along with them. In our business, we had to live and let live. The Dancer turned out to be Rudolf Nureyev. He proceeded to dance around this little table I had in the living room. They finally left after thanking me for playing it and other tapes for them.

In 1956, hi-fi was coming in, and I must admit that setup I had was, in those days, state-of-the-art, and all the tapes I took from the store were really great. I still have most of them.

In the space of ten years, I had done quite well in the music business with major artists and major publishers, and I worked steadily, never being out of work, except for my try at making it on my own.

The Big Three were moving along with some big songs and pictures. In those days, the company got top artists to record the title song of each movie. It was easy to get the play, and the main target was to promote the movie. With artists like Debbie Reynolds, Vic Damone, Pat Boone, and Johnny Mathis we couldn't go wrong, and there was a lot of that in the 1950s. We had a big hit with the Jimmy Dorsey Orchestra doing "So Rare," and Pat Boone singing "April Love," which went to #1. We had a film called *Friendly Persuasion,* and Pat Boone sang that one also, but it was a very hard song to get going. It did well, but was not the hit like "April Love." It was good being a songplugger again.

I introduced Brian Davies to Bob Thiele at a small company called Hanover Records. Thiele recorded some songs with him, but they didn't do too much, and at a later date, Brian got picked up by Dot Records and did a few sides there.

Sometimes, no one really knew who would have a hit record. Larry Stock, a very well-known songwriter with hits such as "You're Nobody Till Somebody Loves You" among others, heard a pre-release of a new record coming out. He didn't like the way the artist did his song with a Rock and Roll beat, so he tried to stop it from coming out, but by the time he tried to stop it, it had become #1. He didn't follow through on his objections, just enjoyed going to the bank. The song was "Blueberry Hill," as recorded by Fats Domino.

My boat was still floating, and so I spent many weekends out on it. Brian, Guy, Bob, and many artists came out and had great times. One day, Mort Fleischmann came out during a low tide. Going down the walkway that moved up and down with the tide, he fell and fractured both ankles. A good time wasn't had by all.

That twenty-six-foot cabin cruiser was built by Elco, the submarine maker. When the tide went out, the boat rested on the bottom because the creek where I docked the boat was not completely dredged out. Sometimes when the tide came back in, the water came in the exhaust pipe and proceeded to fill the boat, it just stayed on the bottom. I always called it a submarine. We re-floated it, took care of the engine, painted it, and off we would go again. It was fun. Barry Kaye, one of my disc jockey friends from Pittsburgh came into New York and wanted to go out on it. He and a small group were having a good time cruising down the East River. I decided to take a shortcut around Randall's Island. I hit something and the rudder was disengaged. I did not have a ship-to-shore radio; I had nothing. We all just went out for laughs. We had them. I dropped anchor, waved my flag upside down, and luckily, some one saw it and called the Coast Guard. They came to us and proceeded to throw us a rope. I tied it up to the capstan, and they started to tow us, but they pulled the thing right out of the boat. We all couldn't stop laughing. Then, they tied us up side by side and took us back. Barry Kaye went on to become a big insurance man and opened his own company selling to the music business and many others. He probably had the most successfully solo-owned insurance company in the world

Gene Block and Shirley came out often and she almost gave birth on the boat. That would have been a first.

Meanwhile we were having some hits at the firm. Vic Damone recorded the title song from *An Affair to Remember,* which went on to become a hit and is still a good standard today. We had a cocktail party on the ship that the movie was filmed on, the *Constitution*. We had a week of screenings at 20th Century Fox Films in New York. We played a dirty trick on everyone. At the end, just as the credits came up, we turned the lights on. There wasn't a dry eye in the place. That picture had one of the saddest endings in the closing scene with Cary Grant and Deborah Kerr. It still chokes me up when I see it today.

In the building where The Big Three had offices, were also the offices of MGM Pictures, MGM Records, and the International offices of MGM. We were on the second, third, and fourth floors, and the Loews State Theater was next to the building. Publishers were all over midtown Manhattan, but the bulk of the publishers were still in the Brill Building. Many other small publishers were at 1650 Broadway. Most of those publishers moved to the Brill Building from Tin Pan Ally when it opened in 1932. Therefore, the Brill Building was really known as "Tin Pan Ally 2."

Most of the publishers had many writers under contract. Those writers used to spend a lot of time at the office writing. Sometimes, two writers got together and collaborated on a song. One of the most well-known writers, Mitchell Parish, the writer of lyrics to such songs as, "Star Dust," "Deep Purple," and many more, had a very strange idiosyncrasy: he would never shake hands or open doors unless he had gloves on. At the offices of The Big Three, he was in the men's room waiting for someone to come in so he could leave behind them without touching the door handle. Bob Jaxon went in, and he knew about Mitchell's idiosyncrasy, so to play a practical joke, he washed and dried his hands, but opened the door just wide enough so that only he could slip through, leaving Mitchell behind him. (He might still be there).

The band remotes that used to be so prevalent were gone by then, and most of our promoting had all gone into radio and television plugs, which is what we called it when someone does your song on a show. The songpluggers were suddenly referred to as "contact" men, and they also had a union. It was really not much of a union, but they had all the publishers sign with them, and we had to be a member of the union to get a job. The union also dictated our severance pay when we were let go. The union had a $1,000 insurance policy for each member, and really nothing more. They also had golf tournaments, so I took up golf. Fred Waring owned Shawnee Golf Club in Pennsylvania. They were usually held there once a year. Every year, Fred invited some celebrities in the business to give out the trophies and also play in the tournaments. Guests such as Jackie Gleason, Perry Como, and Martin Block always came, as well as a few others. They were all experienced golfers, but I was a hacker. They were fun weekends and all free.

One distributor (whose name I won't mention) bet Jackie Gleason a very large bet on their match. It was in the thousands. The distributor lost, and everybody knew about it. He was feeling awful. He didn't have the money and it was a bad situation. Gleason waited until we all were ready to leave after the awards dinner. He didn't announce it, but quietly went to the individual and cancelled the bet. Somehow, we all heard about it later.

The golf tournaments moved to Grossinger's in the Catskills and also the Concord. The change didn't mean much except for the food. In those days, the price of a room included the tee fees, breakfast, lunch, and dinner, and the quality was on par with later cruise lines, or better. The meals were Kosher, but there were many more non-Jews going there. All-Kosher meant there was no dairy with meat dishes. So, leave it to the Jews; they found out about non-dairy milk and used it. They also always had top-notch entertainment, usually a comedian or singer, and it was all included with the cost of the room.

At NBC, which was in the RCA Building that later became the GE Building on 50th Street, the songpluggers used to spend much time on the second floor. During the course of the day, most of us would stop to check the music clearances for all the NBC shows in room 293, which was near where we sat. Also during the course of the day, almost all the artists we contacted came by. There was a large staircase going from the second to the third floor. On the third floor were a few studios, where most of the radio soap operas came from, and some small music shows came from there. *Howdy Doody* was one of the shows in the morning. They played music, and a plug on the show was considered big. Bob Smith was good to all of us. Jack Birch came from a third floor studio. NBC was close, so we spent most of our time there. ABC was uptown and CBS was all over, though most of their shows came from the 52nd Street and Madison Avenue studios, such as *The Arthur Godfrey Show*.

I used to go in and see Mort. His office was on the second floor in the NBC promotions department. NBC also had Guidettes and Guides, who were important to the station. They conducted tours that were informative and also made good money for the network. Many young people tried to become a Guide or Guidette just to get in. They met many artists and show people while escorting groups to the shows and around the building. Also, we always said hello to them. They were warm and receptive.

Many Guides and Guidettes went on to bigger and better things. Johnny Magnus went on to become a top disc jockey. He was a close friend, and I used to know his mother. She used to come in. Joey Heatherton was a Guidette, and her father performed as *The Merry Mailman*, an important show on the air. Robin Watts, who was stationed at the "Bandstand," was a close friend of Mort, and she went on to become an ice skater doing shows all over.

When Mort was doing promotion on the NBC television show, *Bonanza*, he had a promo party at the Concord Hotel in the Catskill Mountains. Stars Lorne Greene and Michael Landon were invited. Mort asked me if I wanted to go. I did, and it was a great weekend. Over the years, I met many of the artists that Mort worked with, including Burt Reynolds, Darren McGavin, Barry Sullivan, Louis Nye, and others.

One day, he and I took two Guidettes, Mickey Overwise and Nancy Howe, to the Friars Club for a few drinks and dinner. We were in the cocktail lounge on the second floor, and at the bar was Errol Flynn. He was drunk, and he tried to pick up Mickey. It was a strange night. Of course, she stayed with us. We spoke with him, and even though he was a little high, he carried on a nice conversation with us and was friendly.

On the sixth floor of the RCA building, NBC had Studio 6A and 6B. Those were the work horses at that time. Morning quiz shows came from them. One show in Studio 6B that we contacted was *Say When*. Carmen Mastrin, a guitar player, used to play our songs. The MC was Merv Griffin. A few years earlier, when Al and I were in business, Merv asked us if we would help a songwriter friend of his and publish her material. We did, but it was just a courteous situation and good will. At night, Studio 6B broadcast *The Milton Berle Show*. *The Tonight Show* with Steve Allen, Steve Lawrence, Edie Gormet, and Andy Williams, came from a theater off Broadway, as well as *Who Do You Trust?* with Johnny Carson. and John Gart was the organist, and he used to play our songs. Those airplays generated good income for the publishers through ASCAP performance credits. When we had no hit songs, getting the play with older songs,(standards), was our job.

At The Big Three, Teddy Black, a good friend of mine, was with Miller Music, and at one time, he was a big bandleader. A few years earlier in 1954, he picked up from a DJ writer "Little Things Mean A Lot," which had been sung by Kitty Kallen, and it went to #1. Teddy and I traveled a lot together, and we usually had lunch in Dempsey's quite often. He was Lebanese Catholic and very religious. We always had fish cakes or Boston Scrod there on Friday. He never ate meat on Friday, so I didn't either, Dempsey's had good fish. The Pope said that people could have meat on Friday, but Teddy stayed with fish, and so did I. Teddy was a good friend of Andy Anka, Paul's father. He introduced me to Sheila, Paul's and Andy's secretary. We went out a few times and I remember she took me out to Andy's house in Tenafly, New Jersey. We spent the weekend there.

Al and Edna were still running the record shop, but places like Sam Goody and the discount houses were slowly killing them. They discounted, but the average record buyer thought he got records for lower prices at the giants. Al was ready to quit, but as things had been going for us, someone wanted him to do well. Al got a call from Mickey Scopp. Mickey was head of The Hummert Radio Features, where Al worked for *Waltz Time* and where he played organ for the soap opera, *Young Widder Brown*.

Mickey had since moved over to The Big Three as General Manager, and he the person who had to OK me for the job, after Norman Foley, okayed me for the Fred Ahlert job. They needed someone to run their foreign liaison office for their foreign branches. Al met with Mickey, and he asked Al why he was wasting his time in a record shop, and then made him an offer. With that offer, it didn't take long to close the shop.

    He started on the new job almost the next day, and a bagel place moved in to his store. I guessed that he had been selling the wrong holes. Al's position started out as the US Representative of Francis Day & Hunter, Ltd., a major London company. He was to be the English publisher's representative in the United States. He had to build the office from the bottom because it was a new operation. The business was changing. With so many small publishers and record companies, the foreign branches became extremely important. Also, picking up songs from those small companies for Europe became big business. This was called "sub-publishing." Al was great at that because we had been dealing with small companies and he knew all the people in the business. Also, with The Big Three, we were a major. Everything worked out well for Al. He established his private office on the second floor, and I was on the third floor.

    David Day was the son of Eddie Day, head of Francis Day & Hunter, Ltd. He came over many times, and he and Al hit it off very well. It was always great to have lunch with them. David used to sweep one pea into a little bit of mashed potato and take little bites, which was probably the right way to eat, but we made jokes about that. He was a great guy.

13

The Second Time Around

1958 and 1959 moved along, and we were working on songs from a number of films, including *North to Alaska* and *Ten Thousand Bedrooms* with Dean Martin. Some were good, and some were not so good. *North to Alaska* had a good title song sung by Johnny Horton, who had just enjoyed a smash hit with the song "The Battle of New Orleans." "North to Alaska" did fair, but sales were not as big as "The Battle Of New Orleans." A film with Bing Crosby and Debby Reynolds called *The Second Time Around* did okay, and we had a couple of songs in that film that were played frequently.

Late 1958, the time came for me to buy a new car again. In those days, new cars came out in September the year before. I got myself a 1959 Thunderbird, which was white with red leather interior. What a car!

Brian Davies got his big break. He read for a part in the Broadway show, *The Sound of Music,* starring Mary Martin. He won the role of the young Nazi in love with the oldest Von Trapp daughter. The musical opened in November 1959, and he obtained tickets for Foley and me to attend the premier, which turned out to be one of the grandest for any Broadway show. In attendance were many celebrities, their names reading like a Who's Who of show business. I had an aisle seat, and sitting right behind me was Ed Sullivan. Brian did the Broadway show for a couple of years, but he somehow did not get the same role in the film version. Joey Heatherton was the understudy for the oldest Von Trapp daughter. After another couple of years, Brian went on to star in the Broadway version of *A Funny Thing Happened on the Way to the Forum* with Zero Mostel.

Lucky Carle and I became good friends. He lived on East 51st Street. In the same building were Johnny Farrow and Jack Newman, both of whom I would work with later on. Also, Andy Ackers, a well-known piano player in the business, and two sisters, Margie and Jane, who worked for record distributors. We were all close, and we enjoyed getting together frequently.

In 1959, Lucky and I decided to vacation together in Puerto Rico, where he had an office. They took good care of us while we stayed four nights far outside of San Juan in a place called the Dorado Beach Hotel, which only cost $15 a night, including breakfast and dinner. A round of golf cost $2 plus 50¢ for a caddy. We played a round with Chi Chi Rodriguez, who was their pro, but he wasn't yet well-known.

We spent the rest of the week in town at the Miramar Hotel. We ate in restaurants all over town. Angel Fonfrias, the Manager of Southern Puerto Rico, took excellent care of us. Lucky was important to the company. He brought in Buddy Holly, and Buddy married Maria Elena, Provi Garcia's niece, who was the receptionist at Southern NY. Provi was from Puerto Rico and was the head of the Latin Department at Southern , and she had much to do with the good care given to us.

Trade Papers

I have mentioned songs and records hitting "the charts." Those charts were listed in trade papers. The first charts back in the 1930s and 1940s were merely lists of songs, and a song needed to have at least ten radio performances to hit the chart that was in the *Brooklyn Daily Enquirer*. The chart was published on Sunday on the entertainment page. To tabulate the chart, the newspaper writer would pick up clearances at the networks and put into a chart all the songs of the week. If a new song had ten "plugs," it earned a spot on the chart. At first, there were only a handful of publishers and they were pushing just a few songs. The more plugs the song received, the higher the song scored on the chart. At that time, the chart listed only the Top 15, but if a song did not receive the required ten performances, it did not hit, so on any given week, there could have been more or less than fifteen on the list.

The charts included the publisher's name, since that was important in those days. At the same time, there was the Peatman List, which was about the same type of listing, but they had all the publishers as subscribers. The Peatman List came in the mail on each Tuesday, and the list also included the weekend performances, so it was more up to date.

Billboard magazine was an entertainment tabloid that had published for more than a hundred years, originally covering traveling shows, circuses, and Vaudeville. They did have a small music page, and it started to get bigger in the 1940s.

Weekly Variety also had a chart of songs and publishers in the Wednesday edition at about the same time. Then, as records gained popularity, the number of trade papers grew, including *Cash Box, Record World,* and *Radio & Records*. The Gavin Report came in the mail from San Francisco. All those trade papers started to publish the play lists of radio stations across the country. They included the DJ's name, or the librarian at the station, or just the call letters.

The fun started when we were told, "Get your record on those lists," and that again began the use of payola. We songpluggers started the use of that word when we called bandleaders "a payola." More and more records came out, and soon, some of those lists began to chart the Top 100. Then, as payola became more rampant, the radio stations started to play only forty records, and they repeated those records over and over again. The trade papers expanded their lists from the Top 20 to the Top 40, which became the trade standard for a few years,

There were Rhythm and Blues charts, Country charts, and Rock and Roll charts, and as a new music genre started, a new chart started. Adult Listening, Contemporary, or Rap; you name it and there was a chart for it. Eventually, the most important list was one that charted how many CDs an artist sells. I think you get the picture.

14

Tossin' and Turnin'

In the spring of 1959, I decided to go to California for a couple of weeks. I had never been there, so, it was a good chance to meet the guys on the west coast who worked for The Big Three. Hy Kanter was the 20th Century guy at Feist, and Eddie MacHarg was the MGM Robbins man. Also, the counter man was Jay Lowey. There was also Barney McDevit, a character and probably the unofficial Mayor of Hollywood. Brian was coming out to meet me where I was staying at the Knickerbocker Hotel.

Kathy Page, who was my first assistant at Santley Joy Music, had become the head of Walt Disney Music Publishers in Hollywood, which wasn't bad for a girl who worked with me at the age of seventeen at Santley Joy Music. She got me passes to Disneyland. I also had a date with someone I picked up at the pool at the hotel. She was the stand-in for Leslie Caron. She looked just like her, and we had a great time at Disneyland. Kathy also reserved a small MG convertible for me.

Barney McDevit took me to the Coliseum to see the Dodgers play on the night when they had an All-Star Game with celebrities. I remember that there was a big tall fence out in left field. They really needed Dodger Stadium.

Of course, Eddie MacHarg took me to the MGM Studios, and Hy Kanter took me to the 20th Century Fox Studios. I had a great time, and was glad that I made the trip. It was good seeing Hollywood in its heyday when the town was not crowded and clean. The Big Three offices were in the Capitol Record Building, which was why we stayed right down the street at the Knickerbocker Hotel.

In 1960, back in NY, I went to the George Burns Friar's Roast. On the dais were Bobby Darin, Myron Cohen, Jack Benny, Al Bernie, Dave Barry, Sid Gary, Harry Hershfield, Ben Hecht, and George Jessel. Ho hum.

The 1960 Dinah Shore Friar's Roast featured Phil Silvers, Joey Bishop, Alan King, Johnny Mathis, Dick Van Dyke, Richard Tucker, Polly Bergan, Red Buttons, Art Carney, Charlton Heston, Ethel Merman, George Montgomery (Dinah's husband), and Jack E. Leonard. It was so great to be a member of the Friars. That dinner was a charity affair, and both men and women were invited to the usually all-male audience.

Over the years, I attended most of the Friar's roasts. They were without a doubt the best affairs anyone could ever go to. The roasting was all done in good humor, and they pulled no punches. They held roasts for Jack E. Leonard (he was his own Roastmaster), Milton Berle, Steve Allen, Jack Benny, Phil Silvers, Lucille Ball (the only female Roastee), Garry Moore, Steve Lawrence, Joey Bishop, Sammy Davis, Jr., Johnny Carson, Harry Belefonte, and Ed Sullivan. I wish I could roll back the clock.

Actually, the first Friar's Club Roast I ever attend was in 1958 for Joe E. Lewis. It was at the Copa in New York, and the cost was $12.50. I took Lonnie Starr, the DJ at WNEW. On the dais were Errol Flynn, Harry Hershfield, Jack Benny, Joey Adams, and Robert Merrill from The Metropolitan Opera. Jack E. Leonard was, as usual, the Emcee. His opening remarks were, "Danny Thomas couldn't be here. He's entertaining the troops in Lebanon. Joey Adams, the illegitimate son of John Quincy. Harry Hirshfield, who refereed the Lincoln-Douglas debate, and Joe E., the only guy in the world who had an honorary liquor license. We have so many "Eyetralians" here, they oughta start a Sicilian B'nai B'rith. And we are surrounded by GAC, MCA, and the William Morris Agency, the enemies of our craft."

The same year, there was a luncheon for Red Buttons, and on the dais were Jack Carter, Buddy Hackett, Mike Todd, Ricardo Montelban, Barney Ross, Jan Murray, and Henny Youngman. Jack E. Leonard introduced Red Buttons by saying, "Buttons was a big hit in *Sayonara*, and then it was released. Because of Buttons, we blew Formosa. Here's Israel's answer to Sessue Hayakawa."

I sat in with William B. Williams, when he took over the *Make Believe Ballroom* at WNEW. He also became a close friend. I proposed him for The Friars Club. I often had dinner with Al Trilling, the head of the WNEW record library, at a place called The Sportsman, a small but comfortable restaurant on 49th Street, where they treated us nice.

I was sitting one night at The Sportsman's bar, and it was during the World Series, when Don Larson had thrown a no-hitter. Sitting next to me was Babe Perilli, who was the umpire in that game. I asked him, "When you got towards the end of the game, were you leaning in his favor and calling the pitches his way?" I immediately wished I hadn't asked that.

Babe responded with an outburst. "He earned it!" he yelled back.

I sunk low in my seat, not knowing what to say.

I did well with Al Trilling and the DJs at WNEW. They could play anything they wanted in those days, but they were influenced by the librarians and tried to stay close to the station's sound. However, I could walk off the street and get a record played there anytime I wanted. Of course, it had to be a halfway decent record. I had carte blanche with Lonny Starr, Jerry Marshal, William B., Klaven & Finch in the morning, as well as others.

There were other DJs in New York, including Jack Lacy at WINS, and the librarian there was Vic Cowen. There was Don Ovens at WMCA, who later went on to head promotions at Capitol Records. All the guys were good to us songpluggers.

In 1960, we continued to work on more movies and title songs. We had another hit with Johnny Horton singing "Sink the Bismarck," which was a strange title for a hit song, but those were the type songs Johnny Horton was doing, and we had the movies for those type songs. We worked the Dimitri Tiomkin score from *The Alamo* starring John Wayne and a great cast. There were a few good songs in that film, including "The Greenleaves of Summer," which did quite well. Also, the album of the film score did well. The film premiere was in London, so John Wayne and Dimitri Tiomkin stopped off in New York while they were on the way. 20th Century Fox set up a cocktail party at the International Hotel right next to the JFK airport. It was an impressive night meeting Tiomkin and shaking John Wayne's hand. He wore his Stetson and he was big.

Also in 1960, Bob Merrill wrote the score for the Broadway show *Carnival*. He was going to audition it for the big wigs at MGM and The Big Three. I was there, and he sang most of the songs with just a piano player accompanying him. We taped it, and I still have a copy of that tape at home. MGM took the show, and I went to the opening in 1961. That was the last thing I worked on at The Big Three.

Norman Foley called me in and he looked quite sad. He had to fire me, even though I was doing quite well for the firm. He said that Mickey Scopp, the General Manager, called him in and told him he was getting pressure from Jack Bregman, the President of another firm that happened to own five percent of The Big Three. He had been told to hire Murray Baker, an old-time songplugger. He had to drop one man to do it, and

Scopp had to figure out who it would be. All he came up with was that I was single and all the others were married. Letting me go was the only way. He figured I could get placed somewhere and could weather being out of work for a while.

I heard about a "new" Puccini opera called *Turandot*. The Metropolitan was going to do it on March 1, 1960, for the first time. I got two balcony tickets at the Tuesday warm-up performance, which was in the old Metropolitan Opera House. It featured Franco Corelli, Birgit Neilsen, and Anna Moffo, among others; but Leopold Stokowsky conducted the orchestra. A few days before, he fell and broke his leg, but he came out to conduct on crutches, which was unbelievable and the greatest opera performance I had ever seen. The audience applauded longer than I had ever heard. They repeated performances on a nationwide, Saturday radio broadcast that was sponsored by Texaco, which I taped, and that version was better than the RCA record that was released of that Saturday performance. The Saturday performance was not as good as Tuesday's. The last act will give anyone goose bumps. Franco Corelli's rendition of Nessun Dorma is probably the best. I like it better than Pavorotti's.

15

Walk Right In

I was out of work. I still ate at Dempsey's every day, made my rounds, and kept looking. Job hunting took some time. One day, Lucky Carle told me he would have a job for me, but I would have to wait a while. Close to six months later, I was ready to give up and move to California. I thought I would have a better chance out there. Things were starting to grow there little by little in the record and publishing businesses. Summertime had little going on anyway, so I was able to last a little longer.

At the end of August 1961, Lucky called me to come up to his office. We then met with Bob Iversen, the General Manager, who was Monique Peer's brother. I was hired to take Lucky's place as head of promotion at Southern Music. Lucky was moving up to become Professional Manager. Before I started to work at Southern Music, they had some great years. They had all the Buddy Holly songs, "The Three Bells", recorded by The Browns, "Georgia On My Mind" by Ray Charles, and others. Lucky was responsible for Buddy Holly, and he was probably the best promotion man in the business. I was happy for the chance to take his place, and, of course, for his great break. Murray Deutch, who he was replacing, was moving over to United Artists Records.

I was back in the Brill Building. Southern Music had the whole seventh floor. They had a big catalogue of Country Western, Latin, Classical, and others.

My first duty was to fire someone, which wasn't easy to start at a new company and tell someone who had been there a while, "You're out." Lenny Meisel, a good friend of mine. I fired him, but told him it came from the top and that I had to do it.

Southern Music had a big staff, including Lenny, Lester Collins, songwriter Sunny Skyler, Lucky, Roy Horton in the Country music department, a few people in the Latin Department, and then me. Everyone knew Lucky and I were close, and even though he was out of promotion and working as the new Professional Manager, we still worked together. He wanted to keep up his contacts. However, I was then handling the east coast and Midwest. They also had a Hollywood office. It worked out fine. We were soon to have some hits, and big ones.

First, they released a Ray Charles album that included "Born to Lose," the back side of the "I Can't Stop Loving You" single. "Born to Lose" made the Top 10. Next, "Tossing and Turning" by Bobby Lewis, a record from Southern Music's England branch that went to #1. "Amor," a Sunny Skyler English lyric that was recorded by Ben E. King was also a hit.

Lucky soon hired an assistant to help acquire recordings, and the normal thing the Number Two man would do. I stayed in promotion. Paul Barry was the first hired.

We were working a few records, including "Granada" by Frank Sinatra, "Lazy River" by Bobby Darin, "One Summer Night" by The Diamonds, "Since I Don't Have You" a remake by Don McLean, "You Can Depend On Me" by Brenda Lee. A few of these were on their way, but they came in and hit when I started. Lucky helped.

I had my T-Bird, and Lucky and I used it on vacations and trips mostly to New England because of all the friends we had there. I remember one trip to Old Orchard Beach, Maine. He had rented a little house with some friends and asked me to go with him. That house had a little screened entrance door behind the kitchen, and there was a window into that area. Every year, the objective was to see how long it took to fill it with beer cans. We almost did it that year. Appearing at the Casino that was out on the ocean was The Tommy Dorsey Orchestra. We went to a place called White's Clambake, where we enjoyed a big steamed lobster, corn, clams, and french fries for $1.25.

On one of my trips to New England, I stopped off at Worcester and met Jim Pansullo, a DJ I had met before in New Haven at WAVZ. During the time between New Haven and Worcester, he married Betty Jo Baxter, a singer recording for Vic Records. In Worcester, they introduce me to their friends and I had such a good I time that I decided to stay overnight. There was a big Italian family that included the Toscanos, the Tomaiolas, and the Pansullos.

Joe and Bertha Tomaiola were opening White Cliffs, a big Italian Restaurant in Northboro that was in a big three-story private house on top of a hill on the outskirts of Worcester. When it was lit up at night, it was beautiful. The food was probably the best Italian food I have ever had.

I soon found out after I told them who I worked for that they were close to Lucky. Tommy Toscano had an Italian grocery store. From then on, I made that my last stop and bought the best Italian prime meat cuts and all my groceries there every time I came through town.

They invited us to spend the 1963 New Year's Eve at the restaurant. Lucky, Jackie, and I went up there. I had a date with Jackie's roommate, Betty. Both Jackie and Betty were English and had real Cockney accents. We remained friends for many years.

Bertha and Joe Tomaiola owned a house in Craigsville on Cape Cod. They always had a big group staying there, but they always found enough room for us.

On other trips to Cape Cod, we sometimes stayed at Ted Black's place near Falmouth but we mostly stayed at the Tomaiola place, but if it got crowded, then we stayed at a motel nearby that was owned by Bob Clayton, who was top DJ in Boston.

Lucky had a temper. Once while we were in the car driving 60 mph, he sat in front with me and Jackie sat in the back. I made a wrong turn and he got so mad he took a swing at me and just barely missed. His temper meant nothing, because five seconds later, he was always over his anger and was as friendly as before.

Renee Schwartz was my assistant. She went on to marry Tony Orlando, but together, we did the mail promo. I started something new after I found out we had our own printing department. I made up 5 x 9 promo cards with a song title and artist name in big letters so that if a DJ threw it out, he still saw the title. We compiled a large, nationwide DJ and librarian list. Those cards went out as soon as a record was shipped. It was a success. Renee did the bulk of it.

My boat was gone. I couldn't keep it above water any longer. I just let it go and gave it to the owner of the boat yard.

1962 brought more big records. "Deep In The Heart Of Texas," a remake by Duane Eddy, "In The Jailhouse Now" by Johnny Cash, "Patricia" by Perez Prado, "Worried Mind" by Ray Charles, and the big one, "You're Nobody Till Somebody Loves You" by Dinah Washington. We heard from DJs all the time. I went on a road trips to the Midwest to meet a few new ones.

Larry Gar was a DJ in Laurens, South Carolina, and he was in the Chamber Of Commerce of his city. I still can't find Laurens on the map, but in those days, the trade papers had lists from a lot of radio stations across the country. The major trade papers in the 1950s, 1960s, and 1970s listed librarians and DJs from almost everywhere, and the more listings a DJ had, the more calls and mail he got, and the more important he became. Larry listed in all the trade papers. He sent his Top 10 in and we always hoped that our songs were on it. He was on our mailing list and got everything from us. I never met him, but we talked on the telephone. We became friendly, and he usually listed me on his lists if I had something.

Every year, Larry sent me five $1 tickets for a raffle for the South Carolina Junior Chamber Of Commerce. For four or five years, I sent in those tickets for the raffle that was held in Myrtle Beach, South Carolina. One dated May 27, 1962 was for a 1962 Ford Thunderbird. The drawing was held on a Sunday. The following Monday morning, I got the call that I had won. I didn't even know the man on the telephone, but he told me, "You won the car!" I had to hear it again. Then I gave out a yell, and the whole office including Lucky and Sunny came running. I told them I won a T-Bird. I am sure that all hell broke loose in South Carolina at the beach when they said the winner was from New York.

Larry told me I had to call a particular Ford distributor and set up a time for when I would pick it up. If you've been following my new car purchases, you know I had a 1959 Thunderbird, and that I liked it. So, I called the distributor who had the car and he told me the car was listed at $5,200. Mine was $3,800, so I guessed that car prices were going up.

I decided I didn't want the car, and I asked the distributor what the value was if I took the cash. He told me $3,800, the same price I paid for my 1959 Thunderbird. I told him I would get back to him. That night, I went down to the bar at Dempsey's where we went at 5:30 p.m. almost every night after work and stayed until at least 7:30 p.m. Everyone met there. It was a great group. We had our own bartender, "Joe the Pro." I asked everyone if they wanted the car. I asked for $4,000, since it would have cost me at least $200 to go down there and pick it up. I didn't hear a peep; no one wanted it. The next day, I called the distributor and told them I would take the cash. In a few days, I got a check for $3,800, which I declared it on my Income Tax. After I took the cash, of course I got a few calls from people who wanted to buy the car, but they were too late.

Meanwhile, we were working more records. I took a trip up through New York State to Albany, Syracuse, Rochester, and Buffalo. In Rochester, I met some great DJs. I mean nice guys, including Ed Meath, Joe Deane, and Dick Biondi and Art Roberts, a couple of guys I got close to in Buffalo. They were at WKBW, a powerhouse station heard almost all over the country. All the cities and DJs had their own thing. In Buffalo, I used to go bowling with Art and Dick. They were in a league I guess, but I also went bowling when I was in town.

I went on another trip with an artist on MGM Records. She recorded a song for us. She was unknown and still is unknown. I don't even remember her name. In Detroit, we stayed at a motel, and I was waiting for her downstairs in front of the lobby. This guy came up to me and started talking, and his friend was also out front. I knew I was in trouble and about to be robbed. I had a lot of cash on me, too. I started talking to him and telling him I was a wounded veteran, and I kept that going for a few minutes. Luckily, a car drove up, and so I said goodbye and walked away. They left, and I was successful. In the car was the local distributor for that artist, and he told me the other guys in the car were going to the Trotters and he would take the singer to the radio stations and I could go along with them to the track. I decided it would be okay. He then said to bet $2 for him on 8&5 daily double. I did. It was the only time I went to the winner's window. His name was Alan Mink. He never gave me the $2, but I gave him the $18.50 he won.

In 1962 Mort went to the Azalea Festival in Wilmington, North Carolina, taking Skitch Henderson, who was to be Marshal. When Mort came back, he said, "I met the girl I'm gonna marry." The girl was Tondea Willis of The Willis Sisters, a trio who performed at the festival.

I threw a lot of Friday night parties in my apartment with Lucky and a few of our friends from Dempsey's. The building wasn't air conditioned, so I put two big window units in, one in the bedroom and one in the living room. They were powerful, and when I put them on together, they sometimes knocked the fuse out down in the basement, and the whole row of apartments on my line lost power on all twelve floors. I never called, since I was sure someone else probably did. No one ever told me to quit using them. That usually happened on a hot night.

I was making ribs one night for about fourteen or sixteen people when the air conditioners went out. Smoke filled the rooms, so we opened the windows, but then the lights soon came back on. It was some night, and the ribs were good. I closed the bedroom door and just ran one air conditioner. All was okay. We used to sit around, sing, and make tapes of our voices. There was Jack Newman, who was a Vice President at Southern Music, and Iversen's assistant. He and his wife, Rona, usually came. Their son, Roger, soon went on and did *The Guiding Light,* and he also became a writer on that show. He came sometimes and he had a great voice. He used to imitate Winston Churchill so well that if we weren't looking at him, we could have sworn that we were hearing the real Churchill.

Mrs. Peer, came to New York from Los Angeles in September 1962. She always stayed at The Essex House. I think she kept an apartment there all the time that overlooked Central Park. She called me to come up with her secretary, Marilyn LeVine. I always called her "Mrs. Peer," and I never called her Monique. Mrs. Peer wanted to meet me. She took over when her husband, Ralph Peer, passed away in 1960 just before I started with the firm. She worked for RCA many years earlier and met Ralph there. She spoke seven languages. I believe she had told me she worked in General Sarnoff's office. When Ralph Peer, Sr. was there, that was the beginning of Southern Music. He went down South and recorded many Country artists, the most well-known being Jimmie Rodgers, who was nicknamed "The Brakeman" because he had worked on railroads and wrote songs about them, and The Carter Family, among others. He put them on RCA Records and they had some big hits. He published the material and that was the start of Southern Music in 1927. Their first song hits included "Blue Yodel," "T for Texas," "Wildwood Flower" by The Carter Family, and "Brakeman's Blues" by Jimmie Rodgers. Ralph Peer, Sr. went all over the south and recorded many artists. Then, a year later in 1928, he left RCA, for his own publishing firm, and Southern Music Publishing Co. was born.

Also in 1928, he had hits with "In the Jailhouse" and "Keep on the Sunnyside." It was the beginning of a dynasty. Ralph Peer, Sr. was a great music man and did well, but Mrs. Peer came into her own with the Latin Department, and she and Ralph were perfect as a pair. They had one son, Ralph Peer II, who became the Chairman and CEO of the company.

Marilyn LeVine and I went up to the Essex House at about 4:30 p.m. and we walked in. I was nervous, but the nervousness soon went away. We talked, and then she ordered dinner in the room. We had a couple of drinks and I was very impressed with her. She was a striking woman, and she knew the business. She also told me she had been following my work and was impressed with me. I was amazed that she knew everything that was happening with the company. I thought she was just a figurehead, but I was wrong. She ran the company. She at once took a liking to me and we hit it off. We spoke about many subjects because I was there quite late.

The office always had a Christmas party at the office in New York. It started around 3:00 p.m. and went on till about 6:00 or 7:00 p.m. The Latin Department had the most fun. We published a lot of the top Latin music. We all always had a great time. Of course the bonus checks were given out that day and made everyone happy.

1963 was to be another great year at Southern Music. I call it Southern because at that time that was the corporate name. It was the ASCAP firm. Peer International Corp. was the BMI Company.

Back in 1941, there was a strike, and the networks would not play any ASCAP music. It started as negotiations broke down over the rates to be charged for the year between the publishers (ASCAP) and the networks. Radio stations started and owned Broadcast Music Inc. (BMI), ASCAP's competitor. I mention this because two major companies signed with BMI, E. B. Marks Music and Peer International Corp, which was affiliated with Southern Music. The Peer International Corp. catalogue had loads of Latin and Country music in it. So 1941 was a tremendous year for the company. A year later, large publishers had firms in both ASCAP and BMI.

In the spring of 1963, Southern Music rebuilt our offices in the Brill Building. We added a studio and the firm was growing. They moved the stock room over to a different building with our in-house printing operation.

Mr. Iversen had me check around for recording equipment. I received recommendations from The Sonocraft Corp., among others. I went over the equipment and ordered it. The cost of all the labor, electronics, and installation was $14,109. Today, the cost would be $30,000 to $50,000. The studio was extremely successful over the years. It had many artists using it and the demos we made of our songs were first class.

Lucky next hired Del Sarino as the Number Two man, however because of the studio, he also worked on demos of new songs and spent much time in the studio.

1963 was another good year. There was a song that came from the Queen Mary out on the seas. Ambrose and his Orchestra were playing a Latin song called "Quando Caliente El Sol," and everyone on the ship was singing it in Spanish. It was a song that Southern Music owned in Mexico. Ray Charles (not Ray Charles the singer) who led The Ray Charles Singers called to see if there was an English lyric and told us why he wanted to know. He happened to be on the ship when Ambrose and his Orchestra were playing "Quando Caliente El Sol." He was going in for a recording session and he wanted to perform the song in English. They gave it to Sunny Skyler, who had written many lyrics to Latin songs such as "Amor," "Besame Mucho," and "Be Mine Tonight," among others. "Quando Caliente El Sol" became "Love Me With All your Heart." Steve Allen recorded it on Dot Records, but it didn't make it. The Ray Charles Singers recorded it on ABC Records and it was released.

Other records released in 1963 "T For Texas" by Grandpa Jones, a Sunny Skyler song, "Don't Wait Too Long," by Tony Bennett, and "Maria Elena, a strange RCA record by Los Indios Tabajaras, two guitar players from Brazil. Unbelievably, "Maria Elena" went to the top on all charts. If you heard it today, you'd ask why, but there it was. We got it played everywhere. Los Indios Tabajaras came to town in their Indian clothes. They were real, and we had a smash. Also a song called "Walk Right In" by the Rooftop Singers went to #1. "Walk Right In" was written in the 1930s. We did not know the writers. Mrs. Peer made us track them down so we could pay them because they never signed a contract and Ralph Peer had taken the song and published it. We found the writers and paid them their royalties.

Jack Newman, the Vice President, came to me with eighteen 45 rpm records, the Southern Library of Recorded Music. He did not know what they were for, but I was told to look into it. He told me that Mrs. Peer told him to give them to me and that I would know what to do with them. I listened to them and it seemed like music for background, commercials, and industrial uses. I found a place nearby called Music Sound Track Service, and I showed them the records. They said they would order them. I then checked and right above them was Corelli Jacobs, a film music set-up. Fred Jacobs was there and he was also interested in the music collection. In a few days, the tapes arrived, and then some 78 rpm records of the same music. I was suddenly in business with a new business. The Southern Library of Recorded Music grew, and I found more customers. With the new material, it became more like a full library and almost a full-time job for me. Users came in, listened, and if they heard something they needed for their project, they took it. They were billed per use, which we called a "needle drop," and we suddenly had a new source of income and another part to my job. There were a lot of industrial filmmakers around the country that needed background music, and there was room for one more library.

About the same time, I got a call from Paul Lazare in Germany. He owned Artist Films, AG, a very large Classical music library. He was coming to New York and wanted to see me. I met him and Inga, his wife, a few days later. He was impressed with our set up, and he wanted me to represent his library in the United States. His library was on reel-to-reel tapes and recorded fantastically well in stereo with The Hamburg Radio Symphony, The Hamburg Philharmonic, and others. He had begun recording in the late 1950s and did most of the sessions during 1960 to

1963. His studio was located in a facility that had once been one of Adolf Hitler's bunkers in Hamburg. We made a deal, and I became his exclusive distributor in the United States, a big selling point for me. He had recorded almost every major Classical piece, and his was the only complete Classical music library around.

The new office layout put each department together. Mario Conti was handling the foreign branches and was with us in the Professional Department, so everyone knew what was happening all over the world and, at the same time, we became a great operation. At that time, Southern Music had twenty-three branches around the world.

16

Love Me With All Your Heart

In October 1964, I made a west coast tour on behalf of Southern Library of Recorded Music. I then had Pat Atanasio as my assistant and secretary. She was responsible and could be left to take care of the Southern Library of Recorded Music and promotion of records on her own. I picked up many clients on that trip. It seemed the production companies and televisions stations were starved for that type of material. I only had a few more than a hundred different records at that time, but they knew there would be new releases for what they needed. I was successful in Seattle, Portland, San Francisco, and Los Angeles. Because of that success, I decided to go on to Phoenix, Denver, Dallas, and Houston. I was successful in those cities, but not as big as in the Northwest. One of my selling points, other than Southern Library of Recorded Music, was the Classical catalog.

In 1964, Mrs. Peer's brother, Bob Iversen, passed away. He had been the General Manager of the New York office and Vice President of the company. His office remained vacant. John Peterson, the Controller, was thinking he had the job and started giving orders, but he ended up not getting the job and it remained unfilled for a while. Ralph Peer II was at Stanford in Palo Alto, and he soon took over. Lucky was not considered for the job. He was doing well in the Professional Department. I had been sending Mrs. Peer copies of everything I was doing. She kept writing me back how happy she was with my work in promoting the Southern Library of Recorded Music nationwide. She kept authorizing me to take more trips to exploit it. Mario Conti was still running the foreign affairs of the company, and assuming many more duties in the office. He was the right man to be General Manager.

Mrs. Peer called me and wanted me to go to Europe, check out the workings of the library with Dennis Berry, the manager of the library in London., and visit all our branches there. On July 3, 1965, I left for London. Then, Dennis and I went to Paris, Amsterdam, and Brussels. I hit it off pretty well with all the personnel, and I met with composers.

Leslie Bridgewater, one of our foremost composers, was playing piano in a major theater right on Piccadilly Square. We were to get there at 10:30 sharp, and we did. We rushed to his flat, and as we walked in, we were amazed to hear his collection of 200 to 300 cuckoo clocks in all varieties chiming at the same time.

In France, we met with Roger Roger, a French composer and musician, who wrote for the Southern Library of Recorded Music. We were invited out to his house for dinner. It was a castle on top of a hill, and all around it was green grass. He showed me around and took me down to his wine cellar. Again, I was amazed at how these people lived. His wife was a singer of opera and all types of music. She was on many of the opera tapes in our Artist Film Library. She sang under many different names, including "Edith Lang," one used in our library

We went upstairs to have dinner. He presented me with a bottle of white wine. Stupid me, I said I didn't think I could carry it with me. He clarified that it was mine to open for the first course. I laughed and so did they. I also proceeded to hold my glass wrong, but I soon learned to hold the glass by the stem for white wines and around the glass for red wines. Later, I corrected people and it made me feel smart. That was when I got the idea to start collecting wines.

The Willis Sisters, a singing trio, came to New York. Their manager, Bernie Brillstein, set up an audition with the ABC Network for them to appear on television on *The Jimmie Dean Show*. They auditioned and were put on the first show. They were so well accepted that they were signed as regulars. At the same time, an audition was set up for ABC-Paramount Records with Sid Feller, their A&R man. The Willis Sisters got the contract and recorded. They had a unique sound, having started singing when they were young, and they had developed their natural, sisterly sound over the years.

When they arrived, they stayed with Danny Winchell, a songplugger and agent, and his wife. Mort, who I mentioned earlier, was going to see Tondea when Danny called him to say that they were going to see a screening of a film. Mort called me and asked if I wanted to go and meet Tondea. I met the three girls, and they were young and cute. I knew Danny before, as he was in the music business and had been around. Not only did I meet Tondea, but I met twenty-year-old Andra, the oldest of the three sisters.

The Dean show changed format and The Willis Sisters only did four shows. However, in the meantime, the girls' parents came up and got an apartment on 72nd Street just off Central Park West, two blocks from me. Mort was then living on West 70th Street and Riverside Drive in The Lincoln Towers. We went to their apartment and saw them. The girls were doing club dates around town. There was a lot of that going on in New York. There were many conventions, and they needed entertainment.

Mort started seeing Tondea, who he said he was going to marry after he met her at the Azalea Festival. He asked me to come along and accompany Andra. We hit it off, and the double dating kept going. The girls started to need spending money, and since the show was gone and their first record had not yet come out, their club dates were just not earning them enough to pay expenses, and living in New York was not cheap. I was able to get two of them jobs at Southern Music, Sheryl in the billing department and Tondea as a clerk.

Southern Music's records were doing well. "Love Me With All Your Heart" by The Ray Charles Singers broke wide open, a hit that was expected. Other hits included "I Can't Get You Out Of My Heart" with Al Martino, "Tell Me" by The Rolling Stones, "Is It True" by Brenda Lee, and a few more.

Andra and I were getting closer and we talked about marriage. I told her we had a big age difference, but that didn't matter to her. We were married in May. Tondea and Mort were supposed to be getting married, but that came later. The girls had a meeting and they said they would keep working and doing club dates. Also, there was a Johnny Carson show set to push their record, as well as a few other shows.

The next year, Sheryl broke up the group. She was homesick after having left her boyfriend, Price McConnell, in Danville, Virginia, which was where they came from. She decided to leave, and that was the end of The Willis Sisters.

Mrs. Peer had "her two Roys," as she called them, Roy Horton, the head of the Country Music Department, and me. We had been working on our worldwide company meeting that was to be held in New York in September. We had just finished rebuilding our offices in the Brill Building and they were to be ready for the large group. An extremely big executive office was built and was to be used also as a conference room. Mrs. Peer told me she was seating me between Han Dunk, our Holland Manager, and Chris Vaughn-Smith, our Australia Manager. She said she wanted me to get close to them. Our Southern Library of Recorded Music was one of the first topics on the meeting agenda.

Ralph Peer, Jr. was still in Stanford, but he was present at the meetings. It was to be his first showing to the worldwide company. When the big worldwide meeting day arrived, Mrs. Peer turned the gavel over to him and he ran the meeting. Many at the meeting did not speak English. You had to see it to believe it. Mrs. Peer was translating from one language to another at certain times, for example Italian to Spanish, German to Italian, and so forth. She was amazing.

We were all given lists of who we would take out. One night, I had the manager from Spain, Mr. M. Salinger, Mr. and Mrs. Brunner from Switzerland, and the Dunks. I took them to Chinatown for dinner, and a good time was had by all. The worldwide meetings lasted a week, and it was great to meet all the branch managers.

There were still many parties in The Brill Building. Louis Prima's office was on the next floor. Tracy, his ex-wife, invited us up to her apartment for a party. I mention this because she lived at 44 Riverside Drive, the penthouse apartment. On the first floor, actors Wally Cox and Marlon Brando shared an apartment. Lucky had all those people visiting him. Mickey Spilane came in once with a gal singer, Sherri Malinou. Mickey later married her. We once went to a party on the upper west side at an apartment shared by Corky Hale and J. P. Morgan. At another party on the upper west side, actors Marlon Brando and Paul Newman were present. We songpluggers were always invited somewhere.

Andra made her rounds. Of the three girls, she was the only one who could read music and play piano, and she was actually the lead of the trio, but she decided to do background singing. She made some good contacts and auditioned for The Ray Charles Singers. She succeeded in getting a regular position with the singers on television's *The Perry Como Show*, but she had to get called for each show because she was a new addition. They soon find out she had a wide singing range and could fill in anywhere. Soon, she was making appearances on *The Steve Lawrence Show* and *The Garry Moore Show*.

We heard that Don McNeil's *Breakfast Club* on radio was looking for a singer. It had to be for a six-month stay in Chicago. We sent a tape of her singing, and she was asked to come out and visit the producers. She learned that Don was leaving the show and Bert Parks was taking over for a while. She got the job on the show.

I made a few trips out there and also make my rounds with the DJs. I met up with Dick Biondi at WLS. He was in Buffalo and became top man in Chicago. We had been corresponding and remained friends. We were talking and he told me they were looking for an all-night man. I told him I heard from Art Roberts and he was looking for just such a job. He was the all-night man at WKBW in Buffalo when Dick was there. Dick called Art, and then he got the job.

Songpluggers were responsible for many artists being discovered, and I had a hand in the helping Dolores Hawkins, Jerry Vale, Norm Prescott, and Art Roberts.

While in Chicago, I decided to stop off at Mercury Records. Morris Diamond was head of promotion. He and I had been friends when he was a songplugger, and he told me that he had just gotten married. He called his wife, Elena, and they invited me for dinner. They lived on the lake shore in a brand new large apartment house complex. He was on a high floor and had a great view of the city.

After returning from Chicago, John Petersen called me into his office and said he didn't think it was a good idea for me to make all those trips to Chicago. I told him I was paying for them and still seeing DJ's when I got the chance. It didn't matter to him, even though I was getting many of our songs on the *Breakfast Club*, which was still a very big radio network show. I was not in a good situation.

17

Mellow Yellow

In 1965, there were more hits: "Can't You Hear My Heart Beat" by Herman's Hermits, "You're Nobody Till Somebody Loves You" by Dean Martin, and the start of a great new artist, Donovan. He was a fresh, new sound for the times, and unbelievable. Lucky and I really didn't understand all the lyrics to his songs, but everyone else did. He first enjoyed three hits in a row with "Catch The Wind," "Sunshine Superman," which went to #1, and "Mellow Yellow," which also hit the top of the charts. The same year, we had "Mas Que Nada" by Sergio Mendez and Brazil 66, We also had two other smash hits, "Winchester Cathedral" by The New Vaudeville Band, and "One Has My Name And The Other Has My Heart" by Jerry Lee Lewis.

Earl Stewart, a friend of Mort's, was a fleet car salesman at a big Chevy agency. I called him, and he pushed the 1965 Super Sport on me, which was a good choice. Earl sold me another car later on. He was the #1 salesman at Chevy and won all kinds of awards. For years, I continued to correspond with him.

Lucky hired a new Number Two man, Jimmie Ienner, who was to stay for some time and do well at his position. Meanwhile, my assistant, Pat Atanasio, who later married, was pregnant and about to leave. She suggested that she wouldn't return, and I had to start looking for someone else. After many interviews, I found Christiana Pierno, and I felt that she would work out fine. She seemed to be a happy person, learned fast, and was able to take over for me while I was away. At the same time, my nephew, Teddy, who was Al's oldest, was coming out of Community College. To tide him over, I was able to get him a position in the stock room and printing department. Also Mario Conti was looking for a new secretary. Teddy's fiancée, Joanne, was also graduating. I got her in, and she was a great addition to the company. In 1964, 1965, and 1966, I had

Sheyrl, Tondea, Teddy, and Joanne working at the company. I should have opened an employment agency and done that for a living.

In May 1966, the final agreement was signed with Artist Films Inc, the Classical music library. Paul Lazare, the owner, still wanted us to represent him in the United States, and our agreement with him would be in force for five years with automatic, five-year renewals unless the contract was canceled by either side. We were authorized to find a label if we want them released. Our main target was to use the music for commercials, television shows, and feature films as background music, and if possible to get them released on records for sale. Paul's Classical music Library that we represented was second to none, and if anyone called for a recording of a rare orchestration, we could usually find it in the library

Paul Lazar became gravely ill in September 1966. I got the call from Inga, his wife, saying that he had passed away and that she was going to take over his work. She was looking forward to working with me. I then got another call from her to correspond with Jan Famira, who she was about to marry, and she said that he would be taking over Paul's work. Then, I got a call from Dennis Berry in London. He had built the Southern Library of Recorded Music, and he reported that he had had no contract with Artist Films Inc., and he asked if I had one. I told him to contact Jan, and I said that I was sure that one would be forthcoming. I had a close association with Jan, and we corresponded often during my travels to Europe, where I had met with him in Hamburg, Germany.

I was then wearing two hats, one representing Southern Library of Recorded Music, and one representing record promotion. That actually worked out fine. I was picking up many new users across the country, and with my DJ trips, I was able to seek out new users for Southern Library of Recorded Music. Many television stations bought the Southern Library of Recorded Music.

Mort had moved to California to run NBC promotions. Tondea made a trip out there to see if she would like it.

We found out that The Lennon Sisters, a well-known singing trio on television's *The Lawrence Welk Show*, were leaving that show after many years. Frank Abramson ran Welk's New York office. Teddy Black and I took Andra's audition tape to him to send to Welk. In October, we got a call for her to come out and sing for him in his office. Welk liked what he heard, and offered her a spot on his show to replace The Lennon Sisters when they left. At the audition, Welk wanted her to immediately join the show.

Roy and Ralph Peer 11 at Stanford University.

    I decide to return to New York. I called Mrs. Peer to see if it would be alright if I came out to Los Angeles to see if the Southern Library of Recorded Music could set up a base operation in California, and then I left for California on November 6, 1967.

    I then planned a trip up to the northwest again. Mort was going up to San Francisco to see Ed Ames, who was appearing at The Fairmont Hotel. I told Mrs. Peer that I was making the trip. She urged me to spend some time with Ralph. I called Ralph, who was still at Stanford University, and told him that I would be in town and that I would like to come out and see him at the university I also invited him to have dinner with us and Ed. He accepted, and he met us at Alioto's at The Wharf. We had a great time, and then we went back to Ed's suite at The Fairmont. It was the first time I had spent any time with Ralph, and since he was actually in the firm, I hoped that we would get close and know each other better. The trip was successful. It was good to again see my old clients, as well as some new ones.

    I returned to New York. During the six weeks I was gone, Lawrence Welk decided that Andra would be a regular on his show. We had a lot to think about. I decided that it would not work out with me in New York and her in Los Angeles, so I decided the move to Los Angeles, the right thing to do.

    I wrote to Mrs. Peer telling her I had to leave the company. I also explained my run in with John Petersen about the Chicago trips, and I told her that it could not be pleasant to stay at the office in NY. I also told her about Andra and her new job with *The Lawrence Welk Show*. In a couple of days, I got a call from her and Ralph saying that they wanted me to stay on, as well as make another trip to the west coast to see if the Library could be moved there. She suggested I do nothing until I saw her. I felt I would be doing the right thing if I stayed on with the company, but that my work should be based in California. I closed everything in New York, but my mom and pop were not happy to hear that news.

18

Sunshine Superman

Leaving Southern Music was not an easy thing for me to do without another job. I was well-liked and probably could have written my own ticket, but I had to do what I had to do. I had made the earlier trip to the west coast to see if the Southern Library could be moved there, and at that time, the choice was right. Other music libraries were also deciding to go there, but those hadn't made a move yet. When I spoke to Mrs. Peer and Ralph on the phone that day, I left the final decision open, saying that I would do nothing until I saw them.

Before I left the New York office, I made sure that Christina Pierno knew the way it should be run, and I introduced her to all the New York clients. She already had been corresponding with the others around the country. I did not want anyone to say I left them cold. Just as I did at Joy Music, I made sure I had the right person in place. I gave my all to that job, and the way I left may not have been on good terms, and I wasn't sure if the Peers would still feel the same when I arrived in California. Al Kugler was to take my place in the Promotion Department, and I showed him around that end of the business. The Peers wanted him for the promotion end of the business, now that I was getting busy with the Southern Library. He would have been a good choice. He was in the printing department and was looking for advancement.

At the same time, the Southern Music office in Hollywood was moving into offices on the fourth floor of the new Max Factor Building that was right across the street from Grauman's Chinese Theater. Their windows overlooked the theater, and since they were expanding the offices, they added another office for me.

New car time came again. I bought a Pontiac Ventura 1967 from Earl Stewart, who had moved over to Pontiac. That was probably my most hated car of all; I just never liked it.

I had been living in the Birchwood Towers in Forest Hills since it opened in 1965, and I called the apartment building office to tell them that I was leaving town. Andra was already in California doing *The Lawrence Welk Show*, and she was staying at Mort's condo in Beverly Hills. I gave a lot of the furniture away and shipped some things to hold in storage until I arrived. I fully loaded the car and left on a Saturday night, driving all night and the next day until I got tired. After driving 1,100 miles, my first stop was at Lebanon, Missouri. I got up very early the next day and drove another thousand miles to Albuquerque, New Mexico. The third day, I again rose early and left, but I had only driven two or three blocks when some lady made a left turn and plowed right into me. She was clearly wrong because there were witnesses and a cop right there. She totaled her car and was hurt quite badly. The whole left front side of my car was banged in. There was nothing mechanically wrong with my car, but the fender was heavily dented. They towed it to a Pontiac dealer, and it took three days to get a fender from somewhere and install the replacement. Time was lost, so I went to the hospital to see the lady. I learned that she worked as a nurse and had just gotten off an all-night shift at the hospital and must have been quite tired when she accidentally ran into my car. She apologized to me, which really wasn't called for, because she was hurt pretty bad. I wished her luck, and since an insurance company soon paid for everything, I was gone.

Finally, I arrived in California. Even with the accident, I was in Los Angeles before the weekend. I went straight to Mort's place. I was glad to be there. I decided I should stay on at Southern Music. I had also heard that Barry Kaye, the DJ who was on my boat, was living in Los Angeles and had started an insurance company. I found out where he lived and called him. When I met with him, he offered me a job with the company. I told him I decided I was staying on with the Peers, if they would still have me. I still liked the music business, and was glad to stay in that work.

On Monday I went to the office as if nothing had happened. The people on the staff were happy to see me, even though they actually didn't know what was going on and I would not tell them until I saw Mrs. Peer and Ralph. The office was beautiful and had plenty of room. Miguel Baca was the Coast Manager and a great guy. He was liked by all.

I often went to tapings of *The Lawrence Welk Show*. The Lennon Sisters were still there, but the show's producers were bringing in new talent little by little. Next to join the show was Tanya Falon, who went on to marry Lawrence Welk's son, Larry Welk. Lynn Anderson was next, and then Sandy and Sally. I became friendly with them all. I also pitched songs as a songplugger would do. I did quite well.

On *The Lawrence Welk Show*, performers were paid the night of the taping of each show. Tanya asked me if I would pick up her check. That night, they were doing a scene where they were supposedly singing from a rooftop. So, I went along the back of the stage where I thought I was behind the set to go to the office to get her check, and I didn't realize that I was walking right in front of a prop sky right into the scene. Since the show was broadcast live, my sudden appearance was not noticed at first by anyone connected with the show. The singing was recorded earlier, and the performers lip synched to those recordings. No one knew it was me, and if they did, I probably would have been barred. They put the blame on Bobby Burgess. I never said a word.

A lot of the talent used to come over to our penthouse apartment on West Knowl Drive, and we had parties and just hung out.

On my last trip to Europe, I was impressed by the people. Of course I will never forget my trip to Roger's castle, and especially my bout with him with wine etiquette and love for good wine. I neglected to say that most of his wines were Bordeaux and they impressed me. When I returned to New York, I did pick up some wines and really started to like them.

Sue Steele, Mrs. Peers' secretary, married Art Clarkson. Art was the distributor of Australian wines in Los Angeles. He soon opened his own coffee, wine, and odds-and-ends store in Beverly Hills. It was a great place. Actually, one of the first coffee and wine places in Los Angeles. He sold coffees from all over the world and, of course, you could drink them there on the other side of the shop. It was two stores put together. He sold wines, and he stocked the good wines. I was in a wine collector's heaven, and he said he would give me good discounts. I picked up Lafite Rothchild 1966, and many other top 1966 wines. I was very lucky that year's vintage was coming in, and they were raving about what a good laying down wine that was. I kept many of those 1966 bottles for years.

We need another car, and so we decided on a 1968 Chevy Camaro for her. I stayed with the Ventura.

Mort married Tondea in August 1967 at Barry Sullivan's house. Mort was head of NBC promotions in Hollywood, and he spent a lot of time with the stars. We were at his place in Beverly Hills for a gathering, and Mr. and Mrs. John Forsythe were there. When we were leaving, they also left at the same time. We decided to stop off at Will Wrights on Beverly

Boulevard for some ice cream. It seemed like nothing to sit with them and just shoot the breeze, and no one bothered us, which is how Beverly Hills was back then.

The office was working out nicely. Of course, the weather there was wonderful and that really was a new feeling for me, a complete new way to live.

I was temporarily sharing Mike Baca's secretary until we decided what we would be doing. I was beginning to really like it in California. Mrs. Peer had a season box at The Hollywood Bowl. It was close to the front, but not too close. Soon, going there began my love for the The Hollywood Bowl. When no one was using the tickets, Sue Steele, Mrs. Peer's secretary, often called me to say that their tickets were available. Nothing was finer than Saturday nights at The Hollywood Bowl for dinner under the stars and good music. I took clients there, but mostly I went with Mort. At a later date, he also got his own box that wasn't too far from us. I later shared his box when I couldn't get the use of the Peer's box.

19

Hurdy Gurdy Man

In 1967 and 1968, I was mainly working on the Southern Library, but still making calls and plugging records. Donovan had several pop music hits, including "Atlantis," "Hurdy Gurdy Man," "Jennifer Juniper," and "Wear Your Love Like Heaven," among others. There is nothing like the feel of a hit song and record, and everyone at our firm was happy. We also had hits with "Little Bit O' Soul," "Soul Coaxing," and a few hits by Herman's Hermits.

When success ran cold, and it sometimes did, our office would feel like a morgue. We just went on and tried again. Getting a record played had become increasingly difficult. Payola was rampant, and unless a record company was behind a record, we had an uphill battle.

The Southern Library had grown, and we had started releasing a lot of the earlier selections in LP form. My move to California was the right thing to do and the timing was perfect. Dennis Berry, builder of the Library, had been against the move. Almost everyone at the firm of any importance was also against the move, but I proved that the change was right. I beat most of the other libraries out there. There was Capitol Productions, and Ascher had a branch there, which opened about the same time I did. The New York library business remained the same with mostly commercials and documentaries, and in Los Angeles, we had film companies, most of whom didn't have their own production libraries.

The reason I mention the studios did not have their own libraries is because of the musicians union. However, a large percentage of them went elsewhere to do the sessions. When a film company wanted a certain piece of music that was not included in the score, they went to library music and it became known as "source" music. That was the main reason I considered my move to Los Angeles the right move; the amount of productions was endless. New York has the same studios and most of them had been my clients for years. New York became just paper work.

Libraries are pre-recorded selections produced to be used as background music, source music, and themes that provide an inexpensive way to include sound-a-likes in film, as well as other uses. Because of union problems, the music was recorded in Europe. If a session was done here, the recordings couldn't be used again in another production, or the musicians had to be paid again. I believe there should be compensation, or it would be very expensive for producers. We tried to reach some kind of agreement with the union, but they flatly refused. We also tried to reach an agreement for demonstration records of songs, but again they refused.

We were pressing our LPs in London, but we soon decided to start pressing in California and save a lot of money. We sold the bulk of them in the United States, and shipping was expensive and took too long.

Production music libraries were important to film companies, television producers, and documentary film houses. There were quite a few sound studios like the earlier ones I mentioned, including Music Sound Track Service and Corelli Jacobs, who also handled a major library out of London called The DeWolfe Music Library. I was very successful in placing our records and tapes with them.

I would have liked to do library sessions here, but it was impossible because of the musicians union. When we did demos in New York and Los Angeles, we got the top musicians and paid them cash.

There was an organization called, The University Film Association. All the schools across the country that had film departments were members. I felt it was a good place to find new editors. When the students left the school and worked for the studios, they would remember Southern Library of Recorded Music, so I joined. They sent me lists of all the schools, and I sent letters to all of them about the Southern Library.

I liked all kinds of music. Anything could be played for me and I would like it. I could actually converse intelligently on any type of music. For years, I got calls from industry people asking me where this or that melody came from. I collected records in many genres, including jazz, big band, singers, pop, classical, and of course, opera. I used to go to the old Metropolitan Opera House on 40th Street between Broadway and Seventh Avenue. I used to sit in the hot balcony where they kept the upstairs doors open during the performance. I saw many of the top singers.

I once took Elaine Malbin to the Metropolitan Opera House. She was an opera singer who had performed on many NBC productions such as "Amahl and The Night Visitors." I was having lunch in the Gateway Restaurant in the RKO Building and was sitting with Irv Braebeck from the

GAC Agency. I told him I had tickets for the opera, *Valkyrie*, that night and I had an extra ticket. He called Elaine, and she said she would like to go. Irv later married her. One of their twin sons went to work with ASCAP and the other went with BMI.

When the new opera house opened, I sent in for season tickets. I was lucky to get two balcony box seats costing $6.50 each, but the seats were in box number 2, and the balcony was on the second floor. We were so close that I could reach down and shake the hand of the singers. In April 1967, Mrs. Peer came to town and I asked her if she would like to go. She went with me and said it was one of her best evenings at an opera. The season seats were on Tuesday evenings, and I kept them until I left New York, and then I passed them on to my mother and father.

In July 1968, I decided to take a week vacation. Andra was appearing with Lawrence Welk at Harrahs in Lake Tahoe, where Mrs. Peer has a house right on the lake. I told her I was going and would see her up there. I went one night and saw the show. Andra had a solo and did one of Southern Music's top Latin songs, "Coo Coo Roo Coo Coo, Paloma." I invited Mrs. Peer to a performance, and of course she liked it. We went backstage and I introduced her to Lawrence Welk.

The Peers had a thirty-two-foot Chris-Craft cruiser on the lake. She asked me to come out one day and go on it. I never drove a twin engine before and I was nervous. The boat was at a mooring about fifty feet from the dock, and she sent me out in a dingy to open it up, bring it in, and pick her up. To my amazement, driving the boat was easy. My boat had only one engine, and that had two. It was easy to steer since I could use the engines to steer the boat if I needed to. We went out and she started to show me the lake and the sights.

I played in the Lawrence Welk golf tournament and I managed to at least finish. We also had dinner at Harrah's home on the lake, and we went out on his speedboat.

Before I left for Lake Tahoe, I received notice that there would be a University Film Association conference in Denver at the University Of Denver. I had decided that would be a good entree to the organization, so I decided to exhibit. They called me and asked if I would give a presentation, which I accepted. As a sustaining member, I was given a section to exhibit and also an evening to make my presentation, after which I had many interesting questions. Most of the students and teachers knew nothing about library music. I was very successful. I attended a few other conferences after that. One was at Loyola in Los Angeles. While at my exhibit, I saw someone I knew coming towards me. It was Bob Merrill, and he was teaching there.

I got the fever to buy another boat after I went on Mrs. Peer's boat. I decided the time had come. I had always heard that the two happiest days in a boatman's life are the day he buys a boat and the day he sells it. I went down to Marina Del Rey, looked around, and saw a 1964 twenty-six-foot Owens Cabin Cruiser for sale. The boat was my size, and it cost $4,800. I took it out, liked it, and bought it. While we had the apartment, it was a good idea to get out and relax on it. We went to Catalina a few times and stayed over at the Isthmus. We once went whale watching, and when we saw one, we went toward it. That proved to be wrong, because the whale came right under us and up the other side. We were lucky. I guess he was just playing. I'll never do that again.

The fall of 1968 was uneventful except for the arrival of Catherine Schindler as Mike Baca's secretary, and also to help me out with my mail.

Mrs. Peer got tickets to The Palladium to a benefit for someone I didn't know, Bill Stewart, a DJ on KMPC whose wife had cancer and was running out of money. Our business was great at helping each other. Henry Mancini was to conduct an orchestra, and Andy Williams and Peggy Lee were to round out the show. Mrs. Peer asked me to go with her. I mention this because at a later date, Bill Stewart and I became good friends after his wife passed away and he remarried Shirley, Gene Block's ex-wife, a close friend of mine. Bill went on to program music that you hear on earphones when you fly on airlines. I used to bring him records and he used them.

Ralph Peer II was still at Stanford University and was running the company from there. Of course, Mrs. Peer still was the head of the company. In 1968, Ralph was running the radio station at Stanford. At a later date, he opened KYTE, his own small FM radio station in Livermoor, California.

At the same time, I visited the Armed Forces Radio and Television Stations (AFRTS). I met most of the people there including Jack Brown, the gentleman who ran it. He is still a close friend of mine. Also at the Station was Bill Stewart, and then to top it off, Bob Crane had a show there, and he brought with him the same equipment that he used in Bridgeport. AFRTS at that time probably had the biggest radio audience of any radio or network station on the air. It was heard all over the world, and getting on their play list was a coup. When I had a hit record, it was saturated, and for a worldwide company like ours, it was important to get the global

1926 Elco Cabin Cruiser *TACET!*

1964 Owens Cabin Cuiser *TACET !!*

New Rael Chris-Craft

plugs. I did well. I became friendly with most people working there behind the scenes. They had yearly golf tournaments, and I was lucky enough to be invited because there were very few other publishers invited. They got the lowest rate on any golf course, and then they had award dinners that were second to none because they were the armed forces. They had a free raffle and everyone won gifts of televisions and the like, and Marlboro Cigarettes gave out a complete package of gifts to all. They had many donations, including the big gift that was donated by Ralph Edwards. They also gave out plaques for all kind of winners, and using the Calaway System, I was a winner a few times. At a later date, those tournaments were picked up by The Pacific Pioneer Broadcasters.

Patsy Garrett was a member, and I became a member when she proposed me in 1968. Almost everyone who was in broadcasting was a member. The luncheon meetings were at The Sportsman's Lodge every six weeks on a Friday afternoon. They honored someone in the business and roasted him or her, such as John Wayne, Bob Hope, Martha Raye, Pat O'Brien, and many more. I would say they roasted just about everyone in the business. They drew anywhere from 700 to a 1,000 members and guests at each meeting. The dais usually had as many big names on it as in the audience. I enjoyed going to those luncheon meetings and the golf tournaments because they were great for seeing other people in the business.

20

Knock, Knock, Who's There?

I stayed on with the Peers, and I was spending more time at the networks in Los Angeles, getting our standards played and also pushing our well-respected Southern Library of Recorded Music. We had a full staff in the Hollywood office, including Mike Baca, the manager, and Denny Diante, the new creative director.

With the birth of Spark Records in the London office, Peer Southern Productions (PSP) began. Denny was to handle PSP from Los Angeles. The first PSP production was actually produced by Elizabeth Waldo, the artist, and Carl S. Dentzel, her husband. Elizabeth was Mrs. Peer's friend, and Mr. Dentzel was the director of the Southwest Museum in Pasadena, California. It had a large amount of California Indian relics. We backed the session, and then we planned to release it in time for the California Bicentennial in late 1969 on our label in the United States that was called PSO Records.

I was involved with the production of the album notes. We had eight pages of drawings by Ted De Grazia, who was an outstanding artist well-known for capturing historical events of the Southwest. His etchings for the album were first rate, and probably worth a lot today because the album is out of print, having only had an initial run of 20,000 records. I was able to keep the original etchings. The album was a great production of Chumash Indian Music, Mexican, Religioso, and Spanish music. "Viva California," the title of the album, was released on time and earned excellent reviews for that type music. The album was a labor of love for Mrs. Peer, but unfortunately, it did not sell well. However, over the years, Catherine Schindler, who took over the promotion and sale of the project, sold all the records, and over the years, it finally did make money.

Also in March 1969, I started to look for a house. I never owned one before because I was strictly an apartment dweller all my life. Mort had moved to Tarzana and had a great real estate Agent. I called her and told her what we were looking for. She took us around and showed us a few. Then one Thursday, she called and said, "Come right out, this one would go fast." We saw it and took it, signing the papers on Saturday. The house was listed for one day and sold the same day, which was good for the seller. It had a pool, and all I could think of asking was, "Does it work?"

We moved in April. I went outside to the back yard and it looked enormous. It was the last house in a cul de sac, so it was a large, pie-shaped half acre with all the property in the back. The pool had a black cover on it. I decided to take it off, and kept rolling it back for so long that I finally had to ask, "When does it end?" It was a forty-four-foot pool, the biggest around, and I couldn't even swim. The steps in one corner of the pool belonged to me; they were my safe domain.

Every Thursday night, I went down to the marina and started the engine on the boat, but that was all. I finally decided to sell it. There was no reason to keep it, since the swimming pool brought us a new way of enjoying life, and the long trip to the boat from Tarzana wasn't worth the time. Home and pool life were different than living in an apartment. Many of the Lawrence Welk singers were coming over to enjoy our pool, and Mort lived just one block away.

Our record sales were lean by the end of 1969, but 1970 started out with a bang. I was seeing all the networks and pushing our standards along with Southern Library activity. The television shows on the air from Los Angeles at the time were with Joey Bishop, Lawrence Welk, Dean Martin, Andy Williams, and a few game shows that used music. We were well-represented. Denny Diante and Lucky in New York were getting new songs on the market, but those took some time getting started. Our hits included a few by Donovan, such as "Riki Tiki Tavi," "To Susan On The West Coasts Waiting," and "Lalena," and "One Has My Name The Other Has My Heart" by Jerry Lee Lewis, "Mule Skinner Blues" by Dolly Parton, and "You Are My Sunshine" with Dyke & The Blazers. It seemed that "You Are My Sunshine" came back every year with a new artist and became a hit. It was written by Jimmie Davis, Governor of Louisiana, and Charles Mitchell, and the song was one of the big Southern Music copyrights.

In February, I made a trip to New York because of Southern Library of Recorded Music problems. My New York representative, Chris Pierno, had to leave the company, and I had to find someone to take over. That wasn't easy since I wasn't there, so it was decided that I handle all billing and licenses for the time being in Los Angeles. While in New York, I got a call that Migual Baca, the Manager of the Los Angeles, had died at his desk in the office. I immediately flew back.

At that time, the Hollywood office personnel included myself, Denny Diante, Catherine Schindler, and Margaret Frankfort, who was the receptionist from the old office on Selma Avenue and actually got noticeably nervous when asked a question. If anyone had a head on their shoulder, it was Catherine. She was Miguel's secretary, and she got in touch with some of the family, funeral arrangements were made, and it was all taken care of.

On March 5, I got an interoffice memo from Ralph. He was in Buenos Aires at our branch there, and he asked me to take over management operations at the office.

We extended the operation of the office to Las Vegas with the hiring of Johnny Farrow, with whom I had worked back in 1947 at Joy Music. He was to contact all artists going through Las Vegas with our material and get plays on the radio stations in Las Vegas. It was a good idea at the time.

In London, they released "Knock Knock, Who's There" by Mary Hopkin. It was released on Apple Records (part of Capitol Records), and it went to #1. Denny found out that the record would not be released here in the United States. We decided to record Andra with the song, as well as look for some other material. Sunny Skylar had a song we were pushing at the time called "I Adore You" ("Adoro"). It was a big Latin hit.

1969 was the year we successfully picked up new clients for Southern Library of Recorded Music. We signed a contract with NBC to use the Southern Library at all the owned and operated stations, a major coup. We were picking up many universities, and I made a few fruitful side trips to the Midwest.

In August 1969, Lucky and Jackie got married. Jackie began working as his secretary when he was with the Peer International Corp., and she later worked for Murray Deutsch and United Artists Records. Murray left and Lucky took over.

Lucky always called people by a nickname, never their real name. He always called Jackie "Ange," which was short for Angel, and he called me "Roy De Goy" because I was never religious, didn't take off on Jewish holidays, and probably spent more hours in church rather than synagogue.

I didn't attend their wedding, but I made the reception dinner at Vesuvio's Restaurant on 49th Street in New York. They had the banquet room and all their friends were invited.

While in town, thirteen of us went to Asti's Restaurant: our friends from Northboro, the White Cliff's people, The Pansullo's, Toscano's, Lucky and Jackie, and others. The check arrived and they gave it to Joe Tomaiolo, the owner of the White Cliff restaurant. Wrong move. He only glanced at it, but he knew there was something wrong. He told the waiter to take the check back and add it up again. By the time he finished, they had knocked off quite a bit. A good time was had by all.

Mrs. Peer and Ralph Peer, Sr. were great lovers of camellias. Park Hill, their Hollywood home, was one of the largest privately owned properties in Hollywood. At one time, they had a bush or tree of every type of camellia ever grown. Ralph traveled all over the world to find a yellow camellia. He came close, but he never found one. Floyd Huddelston was a good songwriter, and I asked him if he could write a song about the camellia, Tomorrow Park Hill, a well-known flower that was named after Park Hill, won many awards, and was probably one of the largest of camellias. I took him up to meet Mrs. Peer and see the place. He said he would come up with something. Floyd wrote "Tomorrow Park Hill," a beautiful song, and his wife, Nancy Adams, recorded it for a possible release on Mercury's Phillips label. I went to the session and the recording came out pretty good. However it never made it. It wasn't the type song that was being played at the time, but writing and recording the song was a nice gesture on Floyd's and Nancy's part.

Andra was still on *The Lawrence Welk Show*, and she was invited to do the Azalea Festival in Wilmington, North Carolina. They remembered when The Willis Sisters did the show. In the parade was David Hartman, who, at the time, was doing morning show on ABC, and our old friend, Harvey Hudson, who was always the Master of Ceremonies on the show. It was a rush thing for us, and we left right after the taping of an episode of the television show. After we got there, Andra got food poisoning and we rushed her to the hospital. She stayed all day, came out just in time to do the parade, and then went on and did the show at night. Harvey really helped us all the way through it. He drove her to the hospital and then treated her appearance at the show with kid gloves. She was well-received, and, as usual, she sang great.

After three years with *The Lawrence Welk Show*, Andra made a few trips with the band and did shows all over the country. When the band came to a town, everyone had to carry their own luggage. She was in the group, did solos and duets, and had to make wardrobe changes, but she couldn't lift her luggage. She approached Welk and told him she couldn't go on the trips any longer. He said she had to or leave the show if she couldn't make the tours. She told him then she had to leave. After three years, Andra left *The Lawrence Welk Show*. The story was picked up by magazines such as *Movie Mirror, TV Picture Life*, and others, but they made me out to be the culprit, saying that I did not want her to leave town anymore and that her home life was more important than the shows on the road. Well, I took the blame, and it became a closed book. Her career took a new turn and grew fast. She became a top background group singer, and also started to get lots of commercials. Ron Hicklin was the top contactor in town. He booked singing talent, and he took a liking to the versatility of her voice.

21

The Impossible Dream

I started working with a new company run by Mitch Leigh that was opened for the publishing of a score he wrote for a Broadway production of *Man of La Mancha*. I called him and told him the story about "Knock Knock, Who's There?" and the session we were doing, and I told him I could record a song for him if he would pay 25 percent of the approximately $2,000 session, which wasn't much in those days. Denny found "I Adore You," another song he thought stood a chance of being a hit. We got Jimmie Haskell to do the session. I had an idea the way I wanted the song done. I wanted her to whisper the start of the song and let it grow, which was my original idea. Olivia Newton John had a monster hit some years later with "I Honestly Love You," which was done somewhat in the same manner.

We rushed the session. Jimmie worked fast and came up with great arrangements of "Knock Knock, Who's There?" and the other songs. The session went smoothly with Denny producing, and everyone was happy with it.

We started showing it around, but there were no takers because they were afraid the new recording would compete with the Mary Hopkin recording of the song, even though we told them that her version would not be released here in the United States. We also heard rumors that someone who had heard our recording, was recording the same song, as well. Denny played our version for someone, and he then decided to cut it with singer Kay Starr. We were up against a wall, and had to get our recording released. I called Eddie Matthews at Paramount Records because he and I had been friends. When I went to see him, I ran into Gene Block, who was then the head of promotion. He liked it and Eddie liked it, and then in walked Brenda, Gene's assistant, who had heard it through the door, and even she liked it, so we thought our prospects seemed promising. "I think we have a deal," Eddie said, but he added that he would be getting back to me later that day and let me know, even though he didn't have a release out right then. He had to look and see what was coming out and when. I told him it has to be a fast release, and that Southern Music and I would be 100 percent behind the record, and we had nothing out here now in the United States.

Eddie called back and said he could get the record out for us with a rush release. I had paid for the whole recording session except for the song my brother put in, and I was virtually handing Southern Music what I thought would be a hit with a guaranteed release and my help with a promotion.

I called Edna Bettler, an old friend of mine in New York, and offered her money out of my own pocket to help with the promotion. She had been around a long time, and I knew the quality work that she did. She was known by everyone, and everyone liked her. She said she would do it.

Paramount rushed a contract for us and we arrived at a monetary advance, but that wasn't important. I called Al Schlesinger, a great guy with contracts, and with his help, we reached a signed agreement with Paramount in August, and they quickly released the record in September. The record started to hit radio station's charts. I sent out my plug cards, which had always proved successful in the past. I had our Los Angeles promo man, Mike Borcheta, helping and taking Andra to the stations. The song started to climb the charts listed in the major papers such as *Variety, Record World, Billboard, Cash Box,* and *The Gavin Report,* which gave it their Pick of the Week.

Along came Kay Starr's version and a recording sung by Liv Maeson, and they also got their versions released. The New York office of Southern Music. called our London office for a few hundred copies of the Mary Hopkin record, which was still not going to be actually released in the United States. I got a call from Al Kugler head of promotion in our NY office saying that I had to coordinate all promotion through him. My own company bit their own nose off, so to speak, to help kill a record.

All three recordings of the same song couldn't make it, it had to be one. We had the better record, which I even thought was better than the Mary Hopkin version. Jimmie had a great arrangement and made it completely different than the Hopkin record. The song, which had been written by Carter and Lewis, the writers of "Can't You Hear My Heart Beat," "Little Bit O'Soul," "Funny How Love Can Be," "Tossing and Turning," and others that were all hits. "Knock Knock, Who's There?" was good enough to stand on its own, no matter who sang it. Our record charted in its début at #40 in *Billboard*. If I had been the head of promotion when the record charted, that was the record we would have worked. The others would have been relegated to also-ran status. Unfortunately, that was as high as it went. They killed it.

The other side of our version of "Knock Knock, Who's There?" was my brother's song, "Change Of Heart," a nice song, but "Knock Knock, Who's There?" received all the attention. I had produced the recording session under the name of the production company that Al and I started back in 1955. It worked for us again, and we sold quite a few copies of the record, earning more than the advance Paramount gave us.

Paramount went on to release "I Adore You" in January. It received initial play and was a pick at a few stations, but the artist wasn't strong enough to push that type of song with all the radio stations. Sunny Skylar, the writer of the lyric to "Adoro," soon moved to Los Angeles and worked out of the Los Angeles office, where he continued to write lyrics and had a lot of hits.

Ralph Peer 11 and Elizabeth were married in 1971 at the Mission Inn in Riverside, California. Elizabeth was from Hemet. The Chapel and the Mission Inn were beautiful. They went on to have three beautiful children, Mary Megan, Elizabeth Ann, and Ralph III. I also went back to New York to the wedding of Al's oldest son, Teddy, who had worked for us in New York, and Joanne, who worked for Mario Conti in the International Department. I understand it was Lucky who finally pushed them to get married. About the same time, Lucky and Jackie had a daughter, Laura.

1971 was a good year for Southern Library of Recorded Music. A feature film, "American Wilderness," had been produced by a small company that created most of the film score from music from our Southern Library of Recorded Music. To this day, when *Variety* lists all the biggest money-making films, it is still on the list.

The Peers decided to move out of the Brill Building to new offices a few blocks north to 1740 Broadway. I also decided on Emily Klinger to handle the Southern Library of Recorded Music in New York. Actually, 1971 was when the Southern Library fully entered into providing music for feature films. There where a few, but no important ones. Many of those features are still regularly shown on television, and the performances earned more money through ASCAP than we received for the synchronization fees. In those days, to get $25 a cue was a lot of money. Later, the fee went into thousands of dollars.

Bright Promise, a new soap opera was going on NBC. At that time, I visited the NBC record library and clearance departments almost daily. I was able to be there when they were listening to music for the new soap opera. For the theme, I was lucky they picked one from our Southern Library, "Nocturne for Lovers," written by Barry White, (who was actually our Bob Kingston, Manager of the Peer Music office in London, writing under a pseudonym so as not to be recognized). *Bright Promise* only lasted one season, but we did well with ASCAP on earnings from the theme we provided.

Warner Bros. Music had an office in the same building as ours in Hollywood. We were on the fourth floor and they were on the tenth floor. One day, I got in the elevator with Ed Silvers, the head of Warner Bros. Music. A few weeks earlier, he had run into Al, in NY, and if I would have Al call, which sounded like an opportunity. Al and Edna come out and stayed with me at our house. That Monday morning, the terrible Sylmar earthquake struck. Half the water in our swimming pool was thrown out, the brick retaining wall near the pool caved in, and there was a huge mess. Our house held well through the quake with no major damage, but there were many cracks in the structure. I looked for Al, but found nothing but a lump of bedding on his empty bed, and I feared the worse. I started calling him in a panic, only to find him at the other end of the house, where he was on the toilet. The quake knocked the crap out of him.

A couple of days later, Al visited Ed Silvers and learned that he wanted him to run the license, copyright, and foreign departments for Warner Bros. Music. Ed knew of Al through his association with Francis Day & Hunter, Ltd. I don't think Al needed much time to think; he took the job. He went back to New York, closed everything up, and moved to California with Edna and two sons, Bob and Matt. Teddy stayed in New York since he was married and worked there.

Al and Edna soon found a Condo on Balboa Boulevard not too far away from us. Al was in the same office building with me again. He fit the job well because he had so much experience doing administration work at The Big Three.

At the end of 1971, I got an interoffice memo from Ralph Peer saying that he and Mrs. Peer were happy with the upsurge of business with the Southern Library. They offered me a 5 percent commission starting January 1972, an extremely nice gesture.

In January 1972, Howard Lucraft, a British gentleman representing *Daily Variety*, came to see me with a letter of recommendation from Dennis Berry. It seemed that Howard wanted to write a story about the Southern Library of Recorded Music. However, when we got to talking, it turned out I pushed for a story about the whole Peer Music. organization. We just had a forty-year anniversary story in *Billboard*, and I thought it could be incorporated in the story of Southern Library of Recorded Music. I hoped to have a long friendship with him.

Howard was a member of The Hollywood Press Club and was that year's President. He said he would propose me as a member. I told him that I was not in the press. They were becoming an entertainment club and changing their charter to open up the roster. I joined and was given a title of "Aide" until they changed the charter. It was a small group and it did seem that it was more of an entertainment group. We met for lunch and dinner meetings at Don the Beachcomber restaurant. Howard was also a member of the Foreign Press, and he and ninety other members were responsible for the Golden Globe Awards.

I had been a member of The California Copyright Conference since 1968. At that time, my membership was important for our business, and we had great dinners at the Hollywood Plaza Hotel. Back then, most of the members were publishers, record companies, and associated businesses, and speakers including many Congressmen.

One of my top clients in Hollywood was Newjack Sound. In fact, they were my first client when I came out in 1966. Newjack Sound was owned by Bob Newman, and John Barber was the manager and also a songwriter. Their studios were right across the street from us, so I spent a lot of time there. I got close to the engineers, and I was getting a lot of commercials from them using the Southern Library of Recorded Music.

In 1971, John Barber did the score for a film called *The Incredible Two-Headed Transplant*. One of the actors was Bruce Dern. John had a few songs in the picture including "Incredible," the title song. It was a good song, and a group called The Leland Four sang it in the film behind the credits. John also had the record released. I asked him if he wanted us to handle the score worldwide and work it for him. He agreed, and we reached an agreement. The picture is still showing on television and is a cult movie.

"Insight," a religious television series, used music from the Southern Library of Recorded Music on nearly every episode.. There was also a Chris Warfield, a film producer, who owned Essex Films that specialized in R-rated films. He had a film editor named Frank Coe, who worked at first out of Newjack Sound, but went on to edit all the Essex films. The Southern Library of Recorded Music was used in possibly fifty or sixty of his films.

Bob Guarino was one of the engineers at Newjack Sound, and we became close. He and I opened our own recording studio on Melrose Avenue called Your Father's Mustache. It had been a sound studio before we moved in, so it was not too hard to fix up. I bought all the equipment, and Bob put it together and ran it. The studio started to do quite well. We did some good sessions, and it had a pretty good sound. Bob was a great guy, but he wanted to move to Portland, so I was left with the studio and no one to run it. I didn't want anyone else other than Bob, so I sold most of the equipment. Steve Stone, a good friend of mine, was with ATV Music, Sam Trust's company, a big publisher. They were building an in-house studio and I was able to sell most of the stuff to them, so I lucked out.(They eventually sold the studio to singer Michael Jackson).

Ron Hicklin, a top contractor for singers, called Andra for a "cattle call" of singers. It seemed they need someone to sing for Olivia Hussey in a musical remake of *Lost Horizon*. Burt Bacharach was composing the score. With all the stellar names in the picture, it couldn't miss. She went to the audition, and Bacharach picked her. She went to his home, where his wife, actress Angie Dickinson met her at the door. Andra practiced the songs with him, and that was the beginning of her work as a background singer for Ron Hinklin. He called her all the time. The session for the picture was at A&M Studios, and she also had to sing a duet with Sally Kellerman, who was also in the picture, but sang for herself. All the singing came out pretty good, but the public was not ready for a Lost Horizon musical, and it was a big flop.

In 1971 and 1972, we only succeeded with a few minor turntable hits. Country music was starting to grow, and we handled a lot of that. We had hits with "It Wasn't God Who Made Honky Tonk Angels" by Lynn Anderson. Jerry Lee Lewis went to the top with "Waiting for a Train," one of Jimmie Rodger's songs. Don Gibson did "Lonesome Whistle," Donovan had "Celia of the Seals" and "Catch the Wind." John Denver did "Everyday," the old Buddy Holly song, and Jody Miller did "There's A Party Going On."

Denny Diante was having a hard time with Margaret Frankfort, our receptionist. She just didn't fit in, and we needed some young blood. So I had to make the decision to retire her. I think she knew and was ready to retire anyway. When Denny started working for us, they didn't hit it off too well, and there were difficulties with a few others. I hired Cynthia Marooney was first and lasted two years before she got pregnant and had to leave. John Barber at Newjack Sound recommended Renee Weiss, a friend of his from a bank in his building. I hired her, and she stayed a few years.

In 1972, we took on a major project for Denny, a documentary film called *Walls of Fire*. The film featured the murals of Siqueiros, Rivera, and Orozco, three great Mexican mural artists, and the film was narrated by Ricardo Montalban. Jimmy Haskell did the score. Denny actually produced the session, but he called me in to help with the sound of the large orchestra because he had only worked with small groups up to that time.

When we got to the studio, the orchestra seated twenty-eight musicians. We were able to record the long, forty-minute score in two sessions. Denny did a great job for his first large session. I decided to stay out of it and let him produce the sessions, and only interfered when asked. He did ask for help in a few spots, and I felt comfortable, but helped only with balancing the sections. Everyone at the session, including the musicians, were also helping and enjoying the music. Jimmy did a great score.

There was a session within the session, a small Mariachi group, and we let some of the musicians leave the studio. The last and closing cue was five minutes long. Jimmy had the music copied as they started the cue, and people were bringing the sheet music in as they were playing. We were almost starting to run over time, but all the musicians except one wanted to continue on without charge, so they shut him up. We went over by a minute, and the last cue turned out fine with just one take.

At the very end, the score called for strange balancing for the French horns and brass. I was coaching the engineer, and he and Denny worked it into a fine, dynamic finale. When we listened to the tape the next day, we were happy. It came out great.

The film was soon completed and we had a screening. Ricardo Montalban was there, and at the end of the screening, he commented, "What great music." The film only showed in Art Houses and played on television on PBS on Cinco De Mayo. The film won the Golden Globe, and was an Academy Award nominee. Viewing the film proved to be a rewarding experience for everyone watching the eighty-five minute *Walls of Fire*.

22

Anniversary Song

My parents had a long comfortable life, and while my brother still lived in New York, we had given them a 50th wedding anniversary party at the Friars Club.

My father passed away in February 1972. His funeral was at the Synagogue where Richard Tucker, of the Metropolitan Opera, was a Cantor. With my love for Opera, it's too bad I wasn't religious enough to go there for regular services and hear him sing. I've always kicked myself for not hearing him sing there. Al and I had to make an emergency trip to New York for the burial on a real cold day. We stayed with my mom in the same third floor walk-up apartment at 216 East 183rd Street that we had lived in back in the late 1920s, and it still looked the same. We made a fast decision to bring mom back to Los Angeles with us, and we dispersed some of her old furniture and closed her old bank accounts.

When we returned to Los Angeles, she stayed with me until she got on her feet and felt comfortable living in her own apartment, one we found not too far from us. She stayed there for a while, and then we found her an apartment for her where many senior citizens lived.

Proving true the old adage that it's a small world, we learned that Brian Davies had an apartment on the same street. He had been living in California for a while. After he met Erika Slezak, an actress on the soap opera *One Life to Live*, they married, and he returned to New York /

In March 1972, Al was a major help with our acquisition of the Warner Bros. Music Catalogue for South America. At the time, it didn't pay for them to open branch offices in those countries, so we arranged a sub-publishing deal that helped both companies. In those days, representation was required in a country in order to collect royalties of any type. Sub-publishing with a firm like Peer Music, (soon to become the name of the complete world wide organization), was good because they had branches all over the world and were the largest worldwide independent publisher. Peer Music eliminated the necessity of dealing with many independents around the world.

Through Al's dealings with foreign publishers when he was with Robbins Music, our firm, Creston Music, was able to sub-publish a song from France called "Adieu Jolie Candy," a minor hit in France. The sub-publisher had the right to create lyrics for the new country if those lyrics had not been written. For the creation of English lyrics, we were able to get a good writer, Arthur Hamilton, who had written many good songs such as "Cry Me a River." He came up with good English lyrics, and he called the song "If It's All I Can Have." Unfortunately, nothing happened with the song here in the United States.

Co-publishing deals and administration deals are two different arrangements. Co-publishing is when one or more writers want to keep their own publishing and enter into a deal with another publisher to handle promotion and other business aspects. A well-known artist or writer can make a better deal. Also, a song can have one or more publishers because two or more writers may have their own publishing company. An administration deal is when a writer or publisher just wants a company like Peer Music. to handle all paper work and collections.

At about the same time, we entered into several co-publishing deals, including one with actress Raquel Welch and her husband. I don't think she had anything to do with the music we were publishing except to show up and take some pictures with us. Nothing ever came from the deal, but I did get to have my picture taken with her. This deal was a good example of the kind of co-publishing deals that often took place in our industry.

Al and Edna were living on Balboa Boulevard in the San Fernando Valley in the same apartment complex as Norm Prescott, my old DJ friend. I was able to help place Norm at WNEW in New York, where he became an important DJ.

Al's youngest son, Bob Kohn, was going to Birmingham High School in Reseda. Bob Kohn met Michael Prescott, Norm's son, and together, the two young men produced *Contract*, a small suspense/thriller film with a script and a small cast including Neil Lieberman, Bob Singer, Bob Kohn, and Bob Saget. When finished, the film needed music, and I came to their rescue. We were able to pick a few things from the Southern Library. For two high school kids, Bob and Michael did a good job, even going so far as to throw one character played by Bob Saget from a roof. (Saget went on to host America's Funniest Home Videos television show, as well as many

Left to right standing: Ralph Peer, Raquel's husband, Raquel Welch,
Mike Borchetta, Peer Promotion man and Roy seated two songwriters.
Sam Sherman, Producer, seated far right.

other film and television appearances.) Norm moved to Los Angeles to work with Embassy Pictures and opened his own company, Filmation. Bob Kohn went on to bigger and better endeavors later on, after he studied law at Loyola University.

Matt Kohn, who was Al's middle son, also studied law at San Fernando Valley Law School. At later dates, I used them both Bob and Matt Kohn for representation in minor lawsuits, and for the record, I paid them both. (I'm still waiting for Bob to pay me for the recorded music I used for their student film.)

Denny Diante who produced *Walls of Fire* was actually hired as US Representative for Spark Records, a label based in London. Bob Kingston, the Manager of the London office, was also running Spark Records, while Lucky Carle was the Professional Manager running all Peer Music. operations in the United States.

Spark Records released their first album with Keith Mitchell, a British artist who sang show tunes. We hosted a nice cocktail party for him at Mrs. Peer's beautiful house in the Hollywood Hills. The living room had a three-story ceiling, and a terrace that opened out to a panoramic Los Angeles view. At the party were plenty of food, drink, and atmosphere, and well as Mrs. Peer's presence. I don't know of anyone who could drink as much as her and not show it (except me). Her swimming pool featured a waterfall and landscaping that resembled a jungle, as well as the ever-present, beautiful camellias that were all over the place. Film studios sometimes tried to rent the place as a setting for outdoor scenes in films, but she would never allow it.

At the Keith Mitchell party, we had invited everyone who worked at trade papers, as well as our distributors and people from radio stations and record stores. Keith was making an appearance on Julie Andrews' television show, which we thought would be a good kick off for the record. The contract with her show stated that Keith couldn't appear on any other television show for two weeks before or after his appearance on her show. We were stuck. The album did nothing. We got some play, but not concentrated. Tony Richland was our promotion man on the west coast. We did get good trade paper coverage, but that just didn't help. Ultimately, his work was difficult to push here in the United States, even though we tried our best.

Another release on Spark Records was a group called Sparrow. The record was produced in London. I liked some of the cuts and we did get some play with it, but not enough.

Back in 1966 when I was in the New York office, I had met Sam Sherman while he was making for his company, Independent International, a small documentary feature film, *The Revenge Of Agent X* (1966), at one of my client's studios. Throughout the film, Sam used music from the Southern Library of Recorded Music. Over the following years, we became good friends, and he went on to make some other major feature films. The first film was done for Bonomo Studios, and Sam was in charge of production. He used the Southern Library of Recorded Music for the complete score. We went on to working on ten or fifteen films together, and he always tried to use top talent. Sam's films included *Girls for Hire, Naughty Stewardesses,* and *Blazing Stewardesses*

Blazing Stewardesses featured Yvonne DeCarlo, Red Barry, and The Ritz Brothers. Most of it was filmed in Palm Springs at a ranch. The film called for some new songs, which we supplied, and they were sung by Yvonne DeCarlo. All the other songs and the score came from the Southern Library of Recorded Music. Mrs. Peer even came down for the weekend and watched the filming, an arrangement I cleared with Sam. I was

Harry Rttz, Roy, Jimmy Ritz, Al Adamson (Director)

able to place five cuts from the Sparrow album into the film. They worked out great, and one of the cuts was played behind the opening titles.

In *Blazing Stewardesses*, there was a scene with The Ritz Bros that called for an "extra," and I was hired because the costume fit me. The scene was a barbecue, where various characters asked for a hot dog or hamburger, but my character asked for a fried egg sandwich. The scene only lasted a few minutes and had my music in the background. Harry and Jimmy Ritz went thru the scene making the egg sandwich, but it ended up on Harry's face at the end of the scene, which also ended the film career of Roy Kohn, future star.

Harry Ritz and I were having breakfast there one morning and I reminisced that I had seen The Ritz Brothers at Loews Paradise in The Bronx back when they had been in Vaudeville in 1932. He then told me that they opened that theater by being the first act to play there.

The second release on Spark Records was "You Gotta Walk It Like You Talk It" by Donald Fagen and Walter Becker, a score from the sound-

Roy, Yvonne DeCarlo, Monique Peer

track of a Richard Pryor film. The music was produced by Kenny Vance. Fagen and Becker went on to become the music group, Steely Dan.

The time came for another new car. I finally got rid of the Pontiac Ventura and bought a Pontiac Grand Ville, a big four-door car.

Around that time, Steve Stone was working at Capitol Records and was the A&R man for Country music productions in Los Angeles. I approached him with some demos we had from *The Lawrence Welk Show* that featured Andra performing Country music, which was her forte. He liked it, and in a matter of time, he signed her. He was able to get a release in time for The Academy of Country Music Awards show. Andra sang with a group outside during the pre-show festivities on the "red carpet."

At the show, we somehow had two seats together and an extra seat, and behind us sat a very young Tanya Tucker. She called Andra "The Singing Lady Outside." We changed seats with her so that she could sit together with her father and someone else.

That year, Capitol sent Andra to the Country Music Association Awards in Nashville. They also had a promo called Fanfair. She was part of it as a new Capitol artist.

I had also told Roy Horton, the Peer Music. Manager of Country music, that I would be there. I spent most of my time with him, and walking around with him was like walking with the Mayor of Nashville. He knew everyone and everyone knew him. The first two we ran into at one of the hotels were Country singers Porter Wagoner and Dolly Parton. They recorded "If Teardrops Were Pennies," which went to #3 on the charts.

We went to shows every night, seeing Country music stars such as Willie Nelson, Waylon Jennings, Ronny Milsap, and a few others. I've always liked Country music, and meeting all the artists in Nashville brought me even closer to it. Those people knew how to live, and everyone was friendly to each other. When they spoke to you, they spoke directly to you, and they weren't looking around at others passing by.

23

Funny How Love Can Be

Andra released a few records on Capitol over the years, but without me. On April 30, 1973, She was cooking dinner while I sat in our den. She said, "I'm leaving." I couldn't imagine where she was going, but then she said, "No, I'm leaving you." Then, it hit me what she meant. There was no leading up to that, and I had thought everything was okay between us. She packed that night and left. I soon learned that she had already taken an apartment elsewhere.

Our divorce did not become final for another six months. I did not contest it, and we had the same lawyer, so it went along smoothly. I didn't even go to court. Soon after, she married her piano player, Larry Mahoberac.

After being single for so long before we married, it wasn't too difficult for me to get back on my feet. My job was solid and I was always busy. Almost immediately, I met Gloria Goncher, someone I saw every day where she worked as the receptionist at Al's company, Warner Bros. Music.

After Gloria entered my life, I did nothing about it for a while, just said hello. In fact, Margo Matthews, a young lady that shared duties with her, liked me more than she did. Gloria never said hello, but Margo did. I passed them every day on the excuse that I was visiting Al, but I actually went to his office to see her. It took a while before I asked her out. I had the Hollywood Bowl tickets on one Saturday, and I asked her to go with me. To my amazement, she accepted. It was the start of something big, but it would take time.

When Andra left, she took my 1973 Grand Ville. I called my friend, Howard Berkowitz, who was then with Columbia Pictures, and I offered him a good deal for the Camaro for his wife. He grabbed it. I bought myself a 1973 Pontiac Grand Prix, which became one of my favorite cars of all time. Andra got rid of the Grand Ville for a Volvo, I think.

In 1973, Lucky Carle left Peer Music. The company went through some changes in New York. However, we in California stayed with the status quo. Denny and I tried to keep us above board. He loved being in a studio producing records, but at that time, we weren't doing much producing. Denny got a few releases out, but nothing that made any noise. We got "Never Never Never" by Shirley Bassey released on United Artist, and "Since I Don't Have You" by Lenny Welch.

I tried everything to make some noise. We owned most of the Buddy Holly songs, so I even sent out a promo release about the fourteenth anniversary of the tragic death of Buddy Holly.

I was contacted by Peter Majewski, owner of The Selected Sound Library in Germany. He wanted us to be their United States representative. The Selected Sound Library was recording quite a lot of material and it seemed impressive. I was able to reach an agreement with him to represent it here. It was a good addition to the Southern Library of Recorded Music, and helped to make me a solid entity into the production library field. His music was recorded well and had a lot of things we didn't have. My clients were glad to get that material, and they started using it right away. It was good stuff. The library that Jan Famira had was 75 percent Classical, and the music was only on tape, never any LPs or CDs. He reached a deal with Majewski to release thirty LPs and CDs with some of the important Classical material. That became a big help to getting the music around. Then, other than a great regular production library of music, we had the nucleus of a good Classical section. Having both libraries helped and did not hinder the Southern Library of Recorded Music. They were completely different, and my clients were happy.

In the 1970s, there were some major films using "source-music." I was well-represented in a few such as *Thieves Like Us, Women In Sell Block 7, Obsession,* which was a Howard Berkowitz film, and *Claws*. We were to go on and be included in many more important films. As we were an independent publisher, those films were important because they generated income. The major film companies had music in house and they did well in performances.

Films that played in theaters were another story. In the 1930s, big film companies such as MGM, Paramount, RKO, and 20th Century Fox, owned their own theaters, and there was a big meeting about paying music royalties to ASCAP. They all decided against it, and through 2010, there is no music performance fee paid for theater showings. In my opinion, that should be changed. They don't own their theaters anymore, and it also hurts smaller companies. Performance payment was always big income for publishers. Eventually, piracy made those payments get smaller, which was why many publishers were forced to either merge, or they were bought up by bigger companies.

Bob Guarino, who I spoke about earlier, had been a good writer, too. He and a friend, Dennis Coates, wrote at my request, some Bluegrass material for the Southern Library. We did a session and it came out great. Dennis got the musicians and he himself played a guitar and banjo. It was to become one of our biggest money makers in the United States.

At a later date, we decided to do a Country album with a sound so basic that it could be used anywhere. That also became a big album. As of 2010, both of those LPs were the best-sounding Country material of all the libraries around. Almost every big television show has used them, including *Saturday Night Live.* More Bluegrass was needed, so we did another half an LP with Bluegrass sounds. That was recorded with the same group and also received well.

I was living alone again in a big four-bedroom house with just two cats. The guest room never got cold because there was always someone staying in it. I had people from London, namely Bob Kingston, Dennis Berry and daughter, Marjorie Murray, and Anthony Mawer/

Mrs. Peer heard about my divorce. She was very helpful. I guess she thought I had a lot of time on my hands. We went out to dinner quite often. She liked good restaurants, of course. We ate at Scandia often. I took her out to the Tail of the Cock on Ventura Boulevard, when Johnny Guarnieri was playing there.

Mrs. Peer also made some dinner parties at home. One of the first was with Bill Ezell, the owner or manager of Alto Communications. They programmed music for all the airlines. Bill Stewart was with him at Alto Communications, but not at the dinner. That dinner really set us up strong with Alto Communications. After that, I spent most of my time with Bill Stewart, since he did most of the work and was also the announcer.

On other nights, Mrs. Peer and I just sat in the living room with the high ceiling and talked about the business. With the departure of Lucky and the early death of Miguel Baca, she had many things on her mind. She asked me about the Latin Department. Provie Garcia was running it and was in New York, but she wanted someone based in California. I recommended Catherine Schindler, who I said was doing most of the work on it anyway. Mrs. Peer soon called Catherine and gave her the promotion. As of 2010, she was still with the firm, coming in once a week as a consultant.

The Southern Library of Recorded Music was moving along well, and the addition of the Selected Sound Library was a big coup. We were getting lots of action with it, and the Southern Library of Recorded Music was doing well, too. One complimented the other, and we were picking up new clients that used the music in feature films and television, which showed up nicely in our ASCAP statements.

In early 1974, Denny Diante decided to leave the firm. He had been unhappy for a while because he was unable to do any studio work. Also, the death of John Petersen in New York was a shocker to everyone because he was running everything. With Lucky gone, Mario was left with his hands full. I had heard through the grapevine that Mrs. Peer had offered the General Manager job to Bob Kingston, who was in charge at the London office. and that he had turned it down because he wanted to stay in England.

On one of my nights sitting with Mrs. Peer at her house, she said to me, "Any position at Southern Music can be yours if you want it." It hit me that she could have been offering me the General Manager job in New York, one I had always thought would be taken over by Ralph. I told her I did not want to live in New York anymore, especially if I had to go there to have any other position. My decision never compromised my relationship with her. I'm sure she understood my point of view.

After Denny left, we had Suzan Kapner, Marti Sharron, Lorraine Rebidas, and a few other people take over the Creative Department, but they only had minor successes.

Lucky Carle called me from New York to say that he was coming out for an interview with United Artists Records, and to ask to stay with me for a while. He, Jackie, and Laura came out and stayed with me while he applied for the job. Denny Diante was also going there with Al Teller to do some A&R work, which was just what he wanted.

With Lucky's move to California, my golf game picked up. We started playing every Saturday on all the Los Angeles courses. When he began working with United Artists Records, I was able to get him in the AFRTS tournaments. He then was invited every year, and that helped him with the people programming records.

Our golf twosome grew over the years to a foursome and we had a few subs, including Stu Schoninger, who manufactured golf clubs, Marty Weiss, a retired bank executive, Nick Alexander, who was Patsy Garrett's husband and a songwriter, and Len Levy, who was a record company executive who went on to distribute films. We played all over, and I must say

I got a little better and was playing in the 90s. I once had an 88, probably the lowest I can remember.

After Lucky met Gloria and they hit it off, he continued his endearing habit of assigning nicknames, and he called Gloria Goncher by the Italian sounding "DeGonch."

In 1973, we placed three pieces of source music from the Southern Library of Recorded Music in Woodie Allen's film *Sleeper*. I received the license application , and they paid for the music, but to this day, I have never hesrd them in the background music of the movie.

24

Lazy River

I was living alone in my house, and since I was always a party guy, I started throwing Sunday pool parties with from ten to thirty people attending, while I did all the barbecuing, made Bloody Marys, and supplied everything. We all enjoyed ourselves, so I decided to have a July 4th party. I invited a few people, but I really wanted to have Gloria over. I asked, and she again accepted. Soon, she started spending her weekends at my house, even though she lived in West Hollywood.

Sometime late in 1974, Warner Bros. Music moved from our building to 9200 Sunset Boulevard, so I often made a trip over there every once in a while.

That same year, we had a big hit record with 'I Overlooked an Orchid" by Mickey Gilley, which went to #1 on the Country charts. As far as pop music went, we were still shooting blanks. It was hard for us to have the right song for an artist, or to find our own artists. Our creative directors weren't having an easy time. At one time or another, they came in and sat with me to ask what they could do to improve the situation.

I made a trip to New York to meet Dennis Berry, and Ralph offered us the use of his apartment, a duplex located right across from the United Nations Buildings. One night, I had just gone to bed at 3:00 a.m. I smelled bacon cooking. Dennis was making himself bacon and eggs for breakfast, and the odor was drifting upstairs.

We spent a few days seeing clients and getting other business done in the office. I stayed on a few days longer and made some rounds of my clients. At NBC one day, I met with Priscilla Blackstone and Bob Geisenger, who ran the record library there and picked music for many shows. *Not For Women Only*, a new series soon to be broadcast, was looking for a theme with a big band sound. I was at the right place at the right time. I mentioned two of our big band swing albums, and from those, the producers picked "Race The Sun," a great melody that had been written by John Scott, one of the top writers working with the Southern Library of Recorded Music. The series hosted by Barbara Walters stayed on for a while, and our earnings through ASCAP were good, as were most network shows.

When Denny Diante left, and we hired Pat Glasser to handle the creative area. We had artists Rick Lisi and Barry Keenan, a couple of writer/artists that had been picked up earlier, and Pat helped fix up their demos. That didn't help, but we tried. We all had faith in then, when no one else did.

I had heard about a disco club called The Point After that was on Ventura Boulevard, and it was run or owned by Stan Richards, the DJ from Boston who also had a television dance show. I went out there one night, and after I said hello, he called over his hostess, Jackie Loughery, who had been Miss USA 1952. She was Guy Mitchell's ex, who had since married actor Jack Webb, who was well-known for the television show *Dragnet*. Again, it was a small world.

In 1975, Ralph asked me to take over the professional activities at our office. We were not getting any releases out with new material. Those were difficult times for me. I was working at the firm in promotion, the Southern Library of Recorded Music, helping with creative work, end then meeting Mrs. Peer at night with nothing genuinely positive to tell her. However, I was lucky enough to have "Brazil" by The Richie Family, a record that was making noise and a big standard that Peer Music. owned. "Brazil" became a monster hit, and everyone was happy at the office. I still felt bad that I couldn't do much more with pop music. At this time, we strongly needed a record company with us to get material out.

The process of taking a song from paper to a record, and then hoping it would become a hit were becoming increasingly difficult. An artist recorded, wrote, and in some cases, published their own songs. I had to find an artist, produce the demo and the session, and then peddle it. All we were able to do was get our standards out with a current sound. In 1975, we had "Big Mamou," which charted at #39, "Funny How Love Can Be," "I'm A Fool To Care," and "What In The World's Come Over You."

Mort Fleischmann had divorced Tondea. January 13, 1975. Mort and I made a trip to Florida. I made it a vacation, but since Mort was the head of RCA Promotion in Los Angeles, he went on business for the opening of the RCA's Space Mountain ride at Disneyworld. Disney made a big thing about the rollercoaster ride that was to be a major attraction. They had cocktail parties, dinners, and everything else, all paid for by RCA, but the best was yet to come. The day they opened the ride, Mort and I rode in the first car open to the public. I will always remember that when I go there and ride the rollercoaster inside Space Mountain.

We then went to Marco Island. A friend of ours, Jerry Bell, was putting on shows and running a theater at a big hotel. Marco Island Airline on which we flew for the short trip was flying on an old DC3. The flight seemed nostalgic because we sat in the front row, and looking back out the window, I could see oil leaking from the engine onto the wing, something those airplanes did back then. The Flight Attendant had a run in her stocking, but, the plane made the flight safely to Marco Island, where we had a great time with Jerry.

Flying back from Marco Island, we were on the same DC3 airplane. It taxied to the end of the runway, turned around, and prepared for takeoff. The pilot revved the engines wide open, released the brakes, and away we went, just missing the treetops. Mort had been a navigator in the Air Force during World War II, so we looked at each other and laughed during the exciting takeoff.

In 1975, Margo Matthews, the young lady working with Gloria at Warner Bros. Music, left to accept a job running the Copyright Department at Irving/Almo Music, the publishing wing of A&M Records, the Herb Alpert firm. She soon called Gloria and asked if she would like to join her. Warner Bros. Music wasn't offering her anything other than her position as receptionist and typist, so that was a good break for her. She became Margo's assistant. Almo/Irving Music was getting hot with The Captain and Tennille, The Carpenters, Herb Alpert, and many more, exactly what I was referring to earlier when I wrote that a publisher strongly needed a record company to get material out.

A&M owned the studio that once was Charlie Chaplin's studio. In fact, the large studio was the Chaplin sound stage, which had a great sound and was used by many companies for recording.

I began to make some contacts with smaller companies. The first was AVI Records, which was owned by renowned pianist Liberace. Ray Harris was President, so I went to see him with my idea to release our Classical music selections with him, hoping that would also open the door for future releases. I was successful in getting twenty-eight LP's from the Famira/Lazare catalogue released, which helped build AVI Records to a well-rounded label.

For several years, Catherine Schindler had been very successful with Vikki Carr and was able to get her to record quite a few things, especially in 1972, when she was able to get her to record "Grande Grande Grande," which was the Spanish lyric that she wrote for our song "Never Never Never." She was also working closely with the many other Latin labels around town. She fit the job of running the Latin Department quite well. She was great with paper work and also spoke Spanish. She had been born in Mexico, but she had lived in the United States for quite some time. Her husband, Jerry, worked as a court interpreter and also spoke German. He was a great guy. They had three great children, and after he passed away, there were several grandchildren.

I was fortunate to spend some vacation time with Catherine and Jerry. The first was a trip to Puerto Vallarta. We drove to the Tijuana airport, and planned to then fly from there to Puerto Vallarta. As we were standing in line to check in, the price of the ticket went up. Also, because Catherine wanted to honor her commitment to us, she made the trip while suffering from pneumonia. She didn't want to ruin our vacations by canceling.

When it comes to languages other than English, I'm a klutz; I just can't learn them. So I had my interpreters with me. Gloria and I also went on a weekend cruise with Catherine and Jerry to Ensenada. Gloria bought a car from Barbara, one of the gals in our office, since she needed one to get to and from work and just wanted wheels. The car needed new upholstery and other upgrades, so Jerry, some weeks later, without Catherine took us to Tijuana, where he had a friend who had a friend. The price started at $200, but we got it for $112. He was good at bartering. He also needed to stop at a market so he could buy some things that he couldn't buy in the United States. He also had some friends who got him cigars.

When we left Tijuana, the car was full. Jerry drove, and when we arrived at the border, Gloria and I looked at each other. I did not want jail time, so I bought two of those clay planter pots they sell at the border and put them in the car. I'm sure the border officer passed us when he saw those. By-the-way, they did a great job on the upholstery.

Another time, we drove with Catherine and Jerry to Puerto Nuevo, Mexico. There were about six or seven restaurants selling fried lobster. There is nothing like it. If you are ever near there, you should go to Puerto Nuevo just below Rosarita Beach and try fried lobster.

25

Mary Hartman, Mary Hartman

Music was considered to be an international language, and for me, music was the way to remember things that happened in my life. We had great songs when I was growing up, songs to help me remember things. Today, I don't think people will look back and pick out a song and remember anything. I may be wrong, but I can't see any rhyme or reason to today's music. I like it, but after the record dies, I can't remember anything it meant or even the melody.

1976 was to be an important year for me. I was at Newjack Sound in early January. I heard them working on a promo spot for *Mary Hartman, Mary Hartman*, a new television show going on the air, and I heard some of my music being used. I said, "That's mine," but the music had another title on it. Our title for the music was "Premiere Occasion," which had been written by Bob Kingston. Then, I remembered having received a call from the office of producer Norman Lear about a show called *Mary Hartline*. I remembered when I was younger there was a show on the radio that had also been called *Mary Hartline*, and I had presumed that show was coming back and sent some possible themes, of which "Premiere Occasion" was one. They had picked it, and I assumed they thought it was written by the person who did the score. I let it go on the air, and then I called Mary Williams, who was handling the cue sheets, and told her it was mine. With a lot of phone calls and checking, their use of "Premiere Occasion" was approved and I then had the theme for a show that was getting rave reviews. Since 1976 the show has come back many times around the world. We and Bob earned quite a bit through ASCAP because *Mary Hartman, Mary Hartman* was on five nights a week. That was a good way to start the year.

At that time, Denny Diante was recording Ferrante And Teicher, a piano duet, performing for an album of film and television music themes, and they were recording with a large orchestra. I called him and asked that he consider using "Premiere Occasion," the *Mary Hartman, Mary Hartman* theme, and they did, placing the song in the new album as the first cut on side two.

Also in 1976, "Premiere Occasion" (the theme from *Mary Hartman, Mary Hartman*) was released by several artists, including a big single by a group called Deadly Nightshade that went to #79 on the charts and got a lot of play. I was able to get a few more versions of "Premiere Occasion" out, one by a friend of mine, Ann Amore, whose real name was actually Anita Higgins, and another version produced by Joe Saracino and featuring a group called The New Marketts that also charted in the 1970s. I considered "Premiere Occasion" a standard to remember.

1976 was a year for updated standards to find success again. "T for Texas," "If You've Got The Money I Got The Time" by Willie Nelson, "A Satisfied Mind," "Wabash Cannonball," and "You're The One" were all Country song hits, but we were getting a lot of "crossover" songs. Crossover means that a song crosses over from being a hit on the charts for one music genre to the charts of another music genre simultaneously.

Anita Higgins had been an award-winning Classical pianist. She had been picked by Walt Disney to write some theme songs, and she had been offered a contract to record with Johnny Green at MGM, but her contracts fell through when she suffered ill health, and then an auto accident forced her to undergo an emergency operation. Dr. Charles Hotter operated on her hands and restored the use of them to her. He wanted her to play again, and so he contacted Mrs. Peer.

Mrs. Peer invited me to dinner one night, and I arrived to find that Dr. Charles Hotter was also her doctor. Anita Higgins and Don, her husband, were their. Don's father had founded Delta Airlines, and Don was an heir. After dinner, we moved to the living room, and Anita was asked to play the piano. She played some good songs she had written, and she played well, her style was "middle of the road" with a Country sound. The task to help her restart her career fell to me, a task I didn't expect. Another dinner was set up for the following week at Anita's house.

Anita and Don Higgins had a beautiful home in the hills overlooking Universal City. Dinner arrived, but the meal had been prepared by Anita's maid, so we were only served cold cuts, potato salad, pickles, and other simple foods. Dr. Hotter was one of the guests, and he had wanted to make an impression on me, so he was livid. After dinner, I heard more of Anita's material, and I thought she had written some good songs.

We published some of Anita's material and tried to push them with artists and record companies, but there were no takers. Anita decided to record herself as a pianist. She got H. B. Barnum to do arrangements and conduct a large orchestra. The songs to be recorded included three of her own, and the rest were standards such as "Cumana" and "Disco Fingers," which she had been playing for years, "Amor," and "Poinciana." I picked two songs just in case they made it, "Premiere Occasion" (the Mary Hartman, Mary Hartman theme), and "Doorway to Paradise," a selection from the Selected Sound Library that everyone liked.

The recording session was completed with no problems. Her recordings were going to be difficult to sell, so I thought of AVI and the possibility of Anita being pushed as a Liberace protégé, a good idea that Ray Harris at AVI bought.

The next major project in 1976 came from Howard Berkowitz, who was then with Columbia Pictures. He called me for some music for *Drive In*, a completed film that was in post-production. When it was finished, the forth reel to the tenth reel was scored with music from the Southern Library of Recorded Music, and it was done so well that no one would have known. A review at the time opened with "Drive-In is a hoot."

My friend, Howard Lucraft, was also a songwriter and a good production music writer with contemporary music He once had his own band in England and also had written for other libraries. I wasn't getting the type of music I wanted out of London or other countries that we needed here, so I asked Howard to do a few things I needed. I was sure he would make money at it, and I was right. Over the years, we did well with the selections he wrote, which was enough for almost a complete LP for the Southern Library.

Meanwhile, I was still in the Hollywood Press Club. We were doing great things. The monies we made from our "shows" were used for down and out singers, and we had a few who needed help. We started "The Big Band Night", and once we honored big band singers, and at the end of that affair, we couldn't get rid of them. The Sportsmen's Lodge in Los Angeles rocked until after midnight. They just sat around in a circle and sang. We had Helen O'Connell, Patsy Garrett, Martha Raye Paula Kelly, Jo Stafford, Helen Forrest, Bea Wain, and a few more well-known band singers. It was memorable.

The Hollywood Press Club eventually disbanded, but the big band and singers nights carried on with Ginny Mancini, The Society of Singers, and Milt Bernhart with Big Band Night. Ginny put on some great nights honoring Frank Sinatra and many more well-known artists, all successful affairs.

26

Do I Worry?

A publisher needs a record company to survive. The only other way is to have a tremendous catalogue of standard songs such as Peer Music. I was trying to cultivate AVI Records, Liberace's label. I approached Ray Harris, the President and backbone of the label, with our Classical catalogue, and then I approached him about *Back to the Bands*, an album done by Dennis Berry, the creator of the Southern Library. *Back to the Bands* had many of the important songs done by famous big bands, and he did sound alike renditions. Among the standards in the album were some important songs copyrighted by Peer Music including "Moten Swing," "Georgia On My Mind," and "Frenesi." The band had top British musicians, and they had produced a great album. Ray heard it and we had a deal with an advance. That was the beginning of many other master recordings that we later had.

There were good and bad aspects to a music publisher of our size that had its own record company. Having a record company for immediate release of a master recording was a plus, but the expense of having a record company was quite high. We had to be prepared to release quite a few records to make it work. The publisher had only one major expense, and that was the overhead costs of an office and staff. Money came in from many sources, including performances, synchronizations, and monies from record companies for sales, among others. A record company paid for the masters, pressings, and shipping all over the country through distributors, and not every record sold. It was always good to have a small record company to release something that no one wanted, but that we liked. A publisher of our size with hundreds of major standards could expect many records from all over to be updated, released, and to make it big, all with no expense to us.

Restaurants in Los Angeles were getting better and growing fast. When I came out there from New York, I went to the name restaurants until I found the good ones. One of my favorites was The Mediterranean, which was on restaurant row on La Cienega, but which closed because diners were too often told "Have a drink at the bar and your table will be ready soon," even though the place was empty. Lawry's Prime Rib, the Steak House, and a Spanish restaurant on Pico called The Matador were among my other great favorites. I got to know Mr. Freeman, the owner of The Matador, who also was involved with NASA. I moved on to the Hungry Tiger on LaBrea and Hollywood Boulevard, where I used to go every night and meet friends at the bar. Most of my friends were in the record and music business, and going there was like going to Dempsey's in New York. The food was good, too. Further down on Hollywood Boulevard was Musso & Franks, another favorite. I had lunch there almost every day because it was a great place to take clients and that restaurant changed the menu daily, even going so far as to print a new menu every day with the date on it.

At the Hungry Tiger, they had "pools" for different important sports activities. They were for employees only, but a few outsiders were let in if they knew them. For The Rose Bow one year, I was able to split half a bet because it was the last space open. It was with the manager. I went home and didn't even know the scores I had. We won, we split $1,000, which I only learned about when I came back in on the following Monday evening and they told me. I bought drinks for all.

Chris Warfield, who owned Essex Films, was soon to open his own studio within his office complex. He took Frank Coe, who was his music editor. Frank was with Newjack Sound and Chris was doing enough films to keep him busy. Essex Films produced some X-rated films, but they were called "soft porn." If you saw what they release today, they would only be considered R-rated. I'm not proud that I was part of that type of film usage, but it was business and it was what our library needed. The more than seventy-five films I did with him usually included complete scores drawn from the Southern Library. When those films played in Europe, there was a performance fee paid to the publisher. In the United States, there was no performance fee paid, unless the film was shown on television. Later with Pay Per View, those films generated quite a bit of performance fees.

In late 1976, Essex Films released *Sex World*, probably the biggest and best film from him up to that time. Bernie Wayne and a friend of mine went to the Pussycat Theater and saw the film, and, a few days later they met me for lunch at Musso's. They raved about the film and said the music score was great. I told them it was from the Southern Library of Recorded Music, but they couldn't believe it. The title song was from the Selected Sound Library and Frank Coe wrote a lyric to it and played over the opening titles. We had it released as a single and it did get some airplay, but not enough. There were also a few other records released of the song. It was a good song and did well for the film. They had an adult film award show every year, but I never went to one. In 1976, *Sex World* won the award for best song of the Year.

Because of *Sex World,* Chris wanted to do a film that would be accepted as R-rated, and he also wanted to do a live score. The first one was *Champagne for Breakfast,* it was well done and featured a large orchestra, but it did nothing and was a complete flop. Peer Music published the score worldwide.

When Ralph Peer made me Professional Manager in 1975, I tried everything to succeed. The idea of getting AVI Records as an easy way to get releases still was my idea, but due to the interoffice memo I received a few years earlier concerning my promo cards, my hands were tied. New York worked on what they wanted. I remember when I was with The Big Three, they talked about the people in Los Angeles being out in left field and on their own. I found that was still going on. My west coast releases meant nothing, so I was basically lying when I told record companies that we had a big promo team. I couldn't mention the corporate jealousy that went on. All I can say is that I tried and did my best. I was always a company man, no matter who I worked for.

I often received calls from people asking if we owned a song, or something like that. To explain what "public domain" (PD) means, let me illustrate by mentioning a call from a lawyer that handled an important singing group. He wanted to know why we licensed a particular song. He told me the title, and I replied that the song belonged to Peer Music. He said, "It's PD," so I asked him to repeat the title. Again, he said the same title. I answered, "It's ours." It was a good three or five minutes before we ended the conversation. The group had used our sheet music copy. Because they used our melody changes and our lyric changes, it stayed ours, and it went on to win a Grammy Award that year. Of course the original was PD, but our writers rewrote it with some changes in the melody and changed one word in the lyrics. Because of those changes, the song was no longer considered public domain.

As Professional Manager, I looked at most of the material that came in, never knowing what I would find. In 1976, in came something from Chicago that caught my ear with both the singing and music content. It was a recording of a group and a singer that sounded good, and I decided to take the plunge and contacted the writers. I suggested they get an LP together and I would see what I can do. The studio date was set. I went to Chicago and sat in on the session. It was going well and the songs sounded good. The main song that caught my eye was called, "Miss You, Babe." The artist was Jeri Faktor and The Backporch Boys, and the recording was done at a main studio in Chicago. At the end of the mix, believe it or not, someone spilled a cup of coffee on the board. It was good that we had finished the session. We never heard anything about it, but I guess they were out of business for a day or so.

I went back to Ray at AVI, and he liked the production. He went first class and had a picture session for the artist and made a nice cover for the LP. We received no promo help from New York, and so another one went down the drain. I've played it many times at home since, and it is still good. At least with the theme from *Mary Hartman, Mary Hartman*, I was able to promote because it was from our library, and we hit the charts with it and forced a few records to come out.

On one evening with Mrs. Peer, we were talking about many things and somehow I mentioned the Hollywood Bowl to her, and out of left field, she said that she hadn't been there in years and would like to go. I told her the tickets were always for any Saturday night and she should go sometime. "We'll go this Saturday," she remarked, meaning that she, Erika (her housekeeper), and me. The great thing about the box that Peer. had was that there was plenty of room. So, Erika made a great dinner, and we spent time just enjoying it. We went to the concert in Mrs. Peer's limousine. Valet parking was not too far from the box. After the performance, Mrs. Peer was greatly relaxed. We left, and as we were sitting in the limousine, she asked for her handbag, but then we discovered that she had left it in the box. I ran back and found the handbag still on the ground next to her seat, which took a great load off my mind.

At another time, she and I went to the Disneyland Hotel for a convention seminar about the cable industry. We stayed overnight in adjoining rooms. She traveled with a vicuna blanket that was so thin it was like a sheet. She had a "Do Not Disturb" sign on her door so the maid would not clean her room, but I made a mistake and left the door between the adjoining rooms open when we left the room for a meeting. The maid cleaned and probably just went into the other room and changed sheets. When we returned, we discovered that the vicuna blanket was gone. Mrs. Peer needed it because of her phlebitis, and the blanket had to be lightweight. The Manager came up and saw that the "Do Not Disturb" sign was still on the door. When we got back to Los Angeles, Sue communicated with the hotel Manager and we got a settlement.

The seminar was very interesting since it was at the beginning of the cable industry, CATV, and Pay Per View. It was always interesting to hear the other side. We made some nice contacts and gave the publisher's side of the performance situation. We didn't speak officially at the meeting, but only to people around us, and I am sure we made it interesting.

I mentioned the California Copyright Conference before. Mrs. Peer used to like to go to the meetings, and she asked some tough questions of some of the people on the panels. I was always amazed at her knowledge. She was one step ahead of others all the time.

Mrs. Peer and I were talking at the house one night and she told me things I don't think she told anyone else. One night out of the blue, she said to me, "Ralph asked me, 'What does Roy Kohn do?' She said, 'You leave Roy Kohn to me.'" I guess the old saying, "Someone up there likes me," was true.

27

Catch the Wind

In 1977, there were remakes of standards such as "Catch the Wind" by Kathy Barnes (Republic Records), "I Love You A Thousand Ways" by Willie Nelson, "In The Jailhouse Now," a big hit for Sonny James, and "Superman" by Celi Bee, a new artist that did quite well. We also had hits with "Walk Right In" by Dr. Hook, "When My Blue Moon Turns To Gold Again," which was a big one by Merle Haggard, and "You Are My Sunshine" by Duane Eddy. Our Country music department did well with those crossover hits.

The Ann Amore session was turned over to AVI records. However, Ray decided to release "Cumana" and one of the songs she wrote, "It's You Again," first as a single. Unofficially I couldn't do much work on the record because "Cumana" was not our song and that was the side that was to receive plugs for attention. We did get her "Amor" released in a few countries, and the song did quite well in Italy, but it never got released here in the United States.

With Anita and Don Higgins' ties to Delta Airlines, we decide to do a commercial for them, hoping for the possibility of it being used. Howard Lucraft got a group of top Dixieland musicians together to make a record of "South," a Peer Music. standard, and Anita, writing under the Ann Amore pseudonym, did the lyrics. "South" came out great and we all felt that the commercial could make a great spot. We sent it, but we never heard back from them, which shows that being on the inside meant nothing.

A company out of Chicago bought Alta Communications, and Bill Stewart was set to run it. He opened an office on the tenth floor of an historical landmark building at 6777 Hollywood Boulevard that had a 360° view of the area. The building was erected at the same time as Grauman's Chinese Theater, and I believe it was done by the same builder. We at Peer Music. soon moved into the same building, completely taking over the seventh floor. We also had the same 360° view. Bill, his wife, Shirley, and I became good friends, and the relationship was good for me because he used all my records on the shows and he was doing most of the airlines. I was able to get worldwide coverage for our records.

When I took Bill and Shirley to the Hollywood Bowl, Shirley picked up a poached salmon with dill sauce somewhere, and Gloria talked about it for years. Bill, Shirley, Gloria, and I went together to all the Academy Of Country Western Music socials, the Big Band nights, and other affairs.

With the success of *Mary Hartman, Mary Hartman*, I thought it was a good idea to get a lyric for the melody. However, I was told not to accept the lyric until some people above me approved it. I contacted Steve Allen's office and asked if Steve would like to do the lyric, but I told him it had to be approved before a contract was signed, and that the lyric had to be accepted and recorded also. He wrote lyrics, but they weren't accepted. His lyrics followed the story of Mary Hartman closely, and were good lyrics, in my opinion. With Steve's name tied to it, the song could have gone far.

In 1977, we had office problems again. Renee decided to leave, and I was to look again for an assistant that could double as a receptionist, as well as take on other duties. Gay Powell came and left, and then another, and another, until we finally met Barbara Cross. She worked just fine and stayed a while. She and her sister were singers who sang together quite often, and, of course, she wanted to pursue her career. She thought that working for a publisher could help her, so she stayed for some time.

One day Kathy Spanberger, came into my office, sat down, and asked me what to do about the fact that she wasn't getting anywhere and wanted to leave. Kathy was a diligent worker and probably could have gone on and done many good things other than just being Ralph Peer's secretary. I told her that Ralph liked her and probably had bigger and better things in mind for her. I told her I had heard years ago that when you leave the firm, they would not take you back. Kathy must have worked something out with Ralph, because she left for another job, and then she returned and became Manager of the Australian office. When Kathy left, Ralph asked Barbara to take her place, and Barbara came to me and asked what to do. I told her it was a good opportunity for her and would mean more money in her pocket. I told her to take it.

I started looking and interviewed a few applicants until late on a Friday. At 4:30 p.m., I met Angie O'Brien, the last applicant. I said, "You start Monday." I didn't even ask if she could type, even though she did type quite well. Angie stayed for a while, did a good job, and liked her work. I have always had good instincts about personnel. I am good at knowing people and probably could have been a good personnel director at a big corporation.

Kathy went on to become Senior Vice President and Chief Operating Officer at Peer Music. What I told her when she wanted to leave was right.

Barbara Cross did not stay with Ralph too long, and after her came Donna Davis, who moved up to the San Francisco area when Ralph moved up there and opened his office in Richmond, California. She soon ran that office.

At Peer Music, we had ladies who worked for us and liked their jobs. They were always helpful and had the company at heart. I can only remember one who did not. We always heard from them after they left, and many came to our parties, or just came up to our office to say hello.

Catherine Schindler was quite naive when she started with us. I never heard her say a word that a child couldn't hear, but she got indoctrinated when Denny was with us. His office was usually open and he didn't care who heard him. I'm not saying it was wrong, but our business was like that. Words flew, and Catherine's office was right across from his.

As for the ladies, at one point we had Christine Richards, Barbara, and Suzan. At 9:30 a.m., we had a coffee break every morning, and Catherine and I had to hear them talking about their previous nights and whether or not any of them had gotten lucky. The friendly banter was done in good spirits, and I think they had a good time just unwinding. Then, we all got back down to business. Everyone was interested in their work and in helping each other out. There was Gay Powell, who had the cutest little daughter. There was Angie O'Brien, who probably weighed only ninety-eight pounds. Suzan Kapner was hired as the Creative Director in the professional Department. She was having a tough time at it, but did her work. We then had Marti Sharron in that position, and she was a hard worker and was close to getting things to move. After her came Lorraine Rebidas, who also gave it a shot.

As for me, I was a jack-of-all-trades. I had started in the business by working in the stock room, went behind the counter as a glorified runner, became a songplugger, ran the recorded library, served as Office Manager, advanced to President of my own record company and President of my own publishing companies, and most importantly, helped the people who worked around me. I helped many people, especially songwriters, artists, and anyone who asked for help. I don't know of anyone who had bad feelings towards me.

28

I'm a Fool To Care

The next few years were to prove uneventful as far as big records were concerned. Standards such as "Georgia On My Mind" by Willie Nelson, "I'm A Fool To Care" by Marcia Ball (Capitol), "Love Me With All Your Heart" by Johnny Rodriguez (Mercury), "Return To Me" by Marty Robbins (Columbia), and "Since I Don't Have You" by Art Garfunkel (Columbia) had updated releases with various artists.

The Southern Library was getting lots of uses. In Hawaii there was station KGMB, which had a large affiliate called Hawaii Production Center. They turned out many commercials for Hawaii, and they were using the library almost exclusively. I had stopped off there on one of my vacations to Honolulu, and they finally ordered the complete library

Our 1977 ASCAP statements concerning performances were quite big. The Southern Library of Recorded Music was doing well with earnings from the theme from *Mary Hartman, Mary Hartman*, as well as "Race the Sun" from the *Not For Woman Only* show. Johnny Scott, who wrote "Race The Sun," was living in England during the time of those payoffs. After that, he moved to the United States and went on to write the scores for North *Dallas Forty, Final Countdown*, and more films. He probably wrote and performed more music in the Southern Library than any other person. A great musician and composer, he played all woodwinds and did a great deal of solo work on music in our library. He became friends with one of my first clients in New York, Music Sound Track Service. George Craig was the owner along with his mother, Teresa, and they were well-known in the business. They were in the same building as Corelli Jacobs, who, at the time, was my second client back in the days when I didn't know anything about music libraries. Many of my future clients came from them. Fred Jacobs ran Corelli Jacobs then, and his son, Andy, later ran it after Fred passed away.

During Suzan Kapner's tenure, she tried, as I told her to do, to find and cultivate songwriter/artists. She was working on Barry Flast, The Runaways, and a manager/entrepreneur named Kim Fowley. He was a well-known character, who put on shows and had everyone around him so that he was always the center of attention while involved with many groups. Suzan was as involved as much as she could be. The backing for her was not there, but it would have been there if she had proven herself. Those things took time, and we didn't have much time.

Things were taking too long to materialize. If we had a hit going, it would have been easier, but at that time, all was going out and not much was coming in from that department. You have to give to get, but we were going through a change in the business, and writer/artists were taking over. Artists talked big figures and recording contracts, and many artists also wanted to have their own publishing companies. It was tough times, and when the Peers wanted answers, it was hard to answer them. There was a famous line at the end of *Gone with the Wind* that "Tomorrow is another day." For us, there was no tomorrow; there was only *now*.

I liked all kinds of music, but rock and pop music began to change around 1977, give or take a few years. The ladies in our office understood the new music, but I found it difficult to pick a song or an artist to work with. To succeed took money, a record company, promotion, and, of course, payola and luck. Things came together for Suzan, but only after she left. From The Runaways came Joan Jett and Lita Ford, and the lead singer, Cherie Currie, went on to become an actress. As a group, The Runaways went on to become a moderate success.

Even though our work with pop music was going through difficult times, the Southern Library was really taking off. We were getting many industrial films and commercials. I picked up many big agencies such as Sandy Corp. and their client, Chevy Motors, Westinghouse Corp., and others. There was Warren Miller Productions, which went on to do many ski films. Warren started using the library in all his early productions. I started doing films with Doug Lackey, who owned a company called New Music. He turned out almost a production every day, documentaries for big companies and industrial films such as McDonald Douglas and others. He also went on to do many important features, and usually used our library for source music. He became a good friend, and later on in 1994, I moved into his building and had an office and studio with him.

In 1977, I found Brad Stanfield, an artist/writer that I thought he was extremely talented. He had his own group and they had a good sound. I took him in and recorded enough material for a complete LP, but then I couldn't sell it. Looking back, he might have been from the old school with conventional-sounding rock songs. I still think I missed the boat with him. He had a great sound, but I couldn't get anyone else behind him.

There was singer Bob Moline, who had been coming up to the office quite often. He had been doing some things for Disney. He wanted to record, but we didn't have the right material for him. His songs were mostly ballads and he needed more up-tempo music. He wrote well, and he was working with Richard Brill, who found a backer to take him in to do a session.

We had a type of music coming out of England called Northern Soul. It were getting a lot of publicity in the United Kingdom, but they it didn't take here.

In 1977, I had requested they release the theme from *Mary Hartman, Mary Hartman* on Spark Records because the song was a worldwide television hit, but even that fell on deaf ears.

Paul Lazare, the builder of the Artists Films AG Classical library had recorded almost every major work, and he had the foresight to record "Peter and the Wolf" with and without the narration. He soon used the great voice of James Pease, so I then had "Peter and the Wolf" both ways. I got the great idea of having Liberace do the narration. I had to sell it to Ray Harris at AVI. He also thought it was a good idea, but he had to sell it to Liberace. In a couple of days, I got a call that Liberace liked it. I then had the words copied and supplied them to Ray with the great master done by our Hamburg Symphony Orchestra. The recording with Liberace was done, and Ray released the album. I guess they sold some copies. I was listed as Associate Producer on the LP. I think Liberace's voice was perfect for it, and it could have been an important LP for him.

Mario Conti, our Vice President Foreign Liaison, called me and said he was sending Suzanne Klee, a singer from Switzerland, out to see me. She was an artist on EMI in Switzerland, but she was looking to record in Los Angeles. She came in with more energy than any three people, and she probably needed a twenty-five hour day. We sat and talked, and she said that EMI in Switzerland was letting her do a session in the United States. I spent some time with her playing some songs that I thought she could do. I then called Steve Stone, who did recording at Capitol (an EMI company) and asked him to meet with her. I told him that she would be recording here and that he would be a good producer for her. She met with him, they hit it off, and a date was set. I was able to get a couple of songs in the session. The first session came out pretty good, but they were only to be released in Switzerland and Germany.

Steve was working out of ATV Music, a company owned by singer Michael Jackson, and, in fact, it was through Steve that I was able to sell my studio equipment to ATV. Also at ATV was a songwriter named Harry Shannon. I didn't know what I was doing at the time when I sent Suzanne Klee to meet Steve. She ended up marrying Harry. There was a great wedding at Sam Trust's house. Sam was President of ATV at the time. Gloria and I were invited to the wedding, and a good time was had by all. I greatly regret that their marriage ultimately ended.

29

What In the World's Come Over You?

Between the years 1977 and 1981, we were moving along as best as we could. We had many releases, but only few got through that hit the charts. "Maybe I'll Cry Over You" by Arthur Blanch, "Shackles And Chains" by the Osborne Brothers, "Superman" by Herbie Mann, "Blue Moon Of Kentucky" by Earl Scruggs, "It Wasn't God Who Made Honky Tonk Angels" by Waylon Jennings, "Since I Don't Have You" by Don McLean, and a big record by Tom Jones called "What In The World's Come Over You." We also pushed a group called Diesel, and "Sausalito Summer Night," one of the songs from their LP, successfully broke out.

In those years, we had many feature films using music from the Southern Library. Quite a few were R-rated Essex Films, but we had other films including *Tinsel Town, Without Warning, The Return, Dr. Dracula, Battle Beyond The Stars*, and *Humanoids From The Deep*. From Paramount, we had a film called *From Cassino to Korea* for which we did the whole score. There were also *Ninja Assassin, Funny Farm*, and *Love Letters*.

Victoria Cooke was doing an exercise class to be sold on video cassette. She was a Playboy Playmate (August 1981). They needed music for the video. In 1982, it was one of the first exercise videos of that type. She came up to the office with her backers or producers and she proceeded to do each exercise at the tempo she needed. I put together two big reel-to-reel masters, and it all worked out pretty well. I say that because they paid, but I never heard whether it came out or not. I never saw the completed product, but the music we picked and timed came out perfectly fine for her needs.

A call came in for music to be used on the *Barney Miller* television show. In the script, cops picked up a porno ring, and they have some of their films and decide to look at one. One of the cops decides to produce a film of the same type. It was me to supply the music. I wonder why? Well all you see are their faces looking at a screen. I picked music that I had used before in such films, and I decided to end it as a comedy by adding in the "1812 Overture" with canons going off. It was a success, and the show still appears on TV today,

On September 5, 1981, the *Wall Street Journal* had a front page story about music libraries, titled: "Need Music To Do Anything By? These Firms Have It." It was a long article and also used quotes from some of us who ran music libraries. I was quoted, and also one of the first references of such music uses was *Mary Hartman, Mary Hartman*. It was a well-written article, and I'm sure it helped all music libraries.

30

Deep In the Heart of Texas

One day in 1981, a client came into our office. I didn't know who he was, but the ladies in the office did. He was looking for music to do a television exercise show. I put together quit a few selections from the library. When he left, they told me that he was on a soap opera, but they also said that he had gained some weight. He was Richard Simmons, and his new show was an exercise show that was to be syndicated and taped at Golden West Television. Somehow, I managed to get quite a few selections on the shows. The shows ran for a couple of years and did quite well. I had selections from the Southern Library of Recorded Music on almost every show, and we did well. Richard Simmons went on to become famous in the diet field and also as an all around character.

In the early 1980s, there were many television shows using source music. I was getting more well-known and could fill almost any type music that was needed. The Southern Library of Recorded Music was well-represented on *Archie Bunker, Different Strokes, Sanford And Son, Lewis And Clark*, and, of course, *Saturday Night Live. Mary Hartman, Mary Hartman* was also still paying for yearly use of their theme song.

Also in the early 1980s, we were picking up many feature films. A lot were R-rated, but there were also others. *Repo Man* was a big hit film, in fact, one of the cult films that played on television for years, and we had a few music selections from our library in it. *Nadia*, a film about Nadia Comanece, the Rumanian Gymnast, had quite a few of our music selections in it. We also provided music for *Tiger Town* for Disney, *All The Right Moves* for Twentieth Century Fox, and a few more.

In the television series *Dallas*, Lucy was having a big wedding in their plotline, a perfect spot for source music. Music from our library was played all through the wedding reception scenes. At a later date, they obtained a license for a video tape release for that important episode.

I decided to do a Mariachi session for the Southern Library, using an authentic Mariachi band, but they had to add a couple of violin players. I made the mistake of leaving that in the hands of the band leader. He picked up a couple of "gringos," high school musicians, who had no feel for the music and probably couldn't read music, either. It came out horrible. I took it in to remix, cut, and do whatever could be done to save it. Still, it sounded like a pick up band playing on a corner somewhere. I was able to sell it just like that—a bad Mariachi band, and believe it or not, it became a big money-maker for our library. I guess Mariachi bands should not sound too perfect, so now you see how much I know. I should have left it sounding the way it was, however I had the music both ways, bad and not so bad. The powers that be in London would not release it in the library, so we just sold it as it was. However with the burning of CDs today, it is just like a regular master and carries the number MQ53, as do all of the unreleased masters in the library. So, when a client got a selection from me and I used MQ53, it was for an unreleased master.

31

The Great Pretender

In 1982, we moved to new offices on the seventh floor of an historical building, 6777 Hollywood Boulevard at Highland, one that was built in 1927 and refurbished. This was the same building that had been used in the original *Superman* television series for the exterior of the *Daily Planet*. They did a beautiful job constructing the inside of our offices and did anything according to our plans. The office was comfortable, and we all liked it.

Bill Stewart and his studios for programming airlines were on the 11th floor of the same building. We spent much time together. One of the first projects I did after we moved was to honor the 50th Anniversary of Peer Music with a complete one hour show for Western Airlines, a top airline then. I spoke to Bill about the project and he thought it was a good idea. Ralph would be interviewed by Bill, who would then play all our standards. Bill was a good interviewer because he had a big show on AFRTS and had been a top DJ on KMPC in Los Angeles back in the days when KMPC was a powerhouse station.

Ralph was receptive to the idea and appeared on the show with Bill, and it came out well. Both Ralph and Bill were good at talking off the top of their heads and answering impromptu questions, and they used no notes except for the list of songs and records. They were quite interesting.

Lorraine Rebidas was in the hot seat as our Creative Director. She was picking up records and cultivated some writers such as Lori Lieberman. Actually, during her stay, we did have some foreign hits here, including "Sausalito Summer Night" by Diesel, and "Major Tom" by Peter Schilling. One of Lori Lieberman's songs, "Turn to Me" was recorded by Maxine Nightingale. Herbie Mann recorded Donovan's "Mellow Yellow," and received quite a lot of airplay.

From Germany came Taco, an artist from whom we expected big things, but he was only to make one hit record, "Puttin' on the Ritz." Taco was very personable and the performance called for him to wear a tuxedo, top hat, and cane. That was the act. He had an interesting sound, and the recording jumped to the top of charts. We worked on it and did a lot for it, even though we did not publish the song. We took him around to visit various radio stations and did a lot of promotional work. One day, while I was with him in his hotel room, a call was placed to Irving Berlin, the writer of "Puttin' on the Ritz," and a time was set up when Mr. Berlin would be in office so Taco could speak with him. We were hoping for a follow-up hit record with Taco. We had some other small releases, but nothing big came from him, which may have been because of the top hat and cane presentation of "Puttin' on the Ritz."

A group named "Russia" was set to appear at The Roxy, a club on the Sunset Strip. Mrs. Peer was invited to hear the band, and arrangements were all set. I planned to take her to dinner at La Maganette, a restaurant near the club, and Jimmy Tuliani, who was the right-hand man for Mrs. Peer, was to drive us in the limousine. She and I were never at a loss for words, but that night at dinner was like pulling teeth for me to carry on a conversation because she was strangely distant. We finished dinner early, and then I decided to drive back to the house. When we got there, I told Jimmy that there was something wrong with her. I didn't think she wanted to even go to the club. He and I decided she should pass it by. Well I was right, because that following Sunday, she had a stroke.

Mrs. Peer remained bedridden for the rest of her life. Catherine and I often went to see her and Mrs. Peer's eyes lit up when we came in, but communicating was difficult. It really hurt me to see her great mind gone. Every once in a while, we had some kind of gathering and they dressed her and brought her down. She was such a strong person. I always thought she would come out of it at one of those parties. I remember one Christmas Party, Donovan came and sang. She seemed to like it and smiled, but she couldn't show much emotion.

In 1979, I ran into a Sherri Weidman at one of the Academy Of Country Western Music meetings. As we were leaving, the valet brought up her car, a 1975 Jaguar XJ6L, my favorite car. I jokingly yelled to her, "I'll give you $3,000 for it!" She laughed, but I kept in touch with her. In June 1983, she called me to say that she was moving to Nashville and asked if I still wanted the car for $3,000, and I agreed to buy the car right then over the phone.

My neighbors, Vic and Mimi, Gloria, and I drove down to Sherri's house in San Pedro. I didn't even drive the Jaguar, but those cars had a long life and they all looked alike. I gave her a check and started to leave, but then I looked at the speedometer and saw that the car had logged 152,000 miles. It was racing green and did look good. I ran that Jaguar up to almost 300,000 miles.

At about the same time, my brother also gave me his 1967 Ford Galaxy convertible that had crossed the country five or six times. That speedometer had logged only 132,000 miles. It ran great also, but never passed a gas station without stopping.

I sold the Grand Prix to a golfing friend for $1,100. He gave me a check. Then, a few weeks after, he borrowed back the $1,100, and he never paid it back.

In 1984, Universal Studios called us for some big band sounds for *Repo Man*, a major film starring Charlie Sheen that was soon to be released, and we were successful in getting a few songs in it. *Repo Man* showed on television for years and did well.

In 1983, a film producer came into my office needing some Classical music selections, among others, for his film, *El Norte*. He was out of money and asked for help. So for the minimum, I give him the selections. *El Norte* became a major film, and the producer went all over the world and told how he ran out of money, but got the film completed. Since that day, I had a double license. If a project was a budget film, I split the fee so they paid one third up front, but if the film grossed $5 million dollars, they paid the balance. That agreement kept me in business and helped producers. From 1982 to 1984, I was able to be represented in many feature films and television shows.

In April 1985, Ralph called me in to his office and said that he had tentatively sold the Southern Library of Recorded Music to Associated Productions Music (APM). I was to go there and work for them. APM was the largest of all the music library companies, but the sale hit me right between the eyes. Ralph said that I would get severance pay, two weeks for each year I was with the firm, and I would just move over there. I didn't know what to say because I didn't expect that. Looking back, I saw that the reason was that they were cutting down, and I believe there were some others besides me who were leaving. I asked him to give me some time to come up with another idea. I told him I couldn't see myself starting over at another company at that time in my life. He gave me some time to come up with another idea. So, there I was telling the boss that he couldn't fire me.

I spoke with everyone, but only Ken Gerstenfeld, my accountant, helped me arrive at the right decision. He pointed out that there were few other places I could work where everything was in place, product, clients, and the well-known name of Southern Library were all set up ready to go with no major investment from me.

I made an appointment with Ralph and told him I would take it over and do it myself. He said he would work on it and come up with a proposal. I did the same. In a few weeks, we concluded that he would advance me a weekly "salary," and I would pay all my expenses. That arrangement was to begin in September 1985. I immediately asked for a raise, but was turned down. I also never got the severance pay.

Our British company, Southern Library of Recorded Music had never opened here, and was just a subsidiary of Southern Music Publishing Company. I then opened the company here, and when I said "Southern Library," I referred to an American company with Roy Kohn doing business as "Southern Library."

The split actually started before September 1985, but I moved into my new office in September on the second floor of the same building. In that way, I stayed close to the office because I was basically still with Peer Music, but as an agent for them. Ralph also gave me permission to use the Peer Music. office, for which I always thanked him.

The library did well and I started to pick up some major films, such as *Police Academy 2*. That film was a perfect example of how source music was used. There is a scene in *Police Academy 2* that was set in a gay bar. No music was written for it, and they needed music like a tango for the action. In the finished film, "Tango Juanito," the music you hear in the background throughout the scene, came from our Selected Sound Library.

Over the years, there were seven *Police Academy* sequel films. Since I had an office in the same building as Doug Lackey, a music editor, who did most of the sequels, and using my music throughout *Police Academy 7: Mission to Moscow*." I think all the scores were written by Robert Folk. Robert came up to see me when he first came to town, and he wanted to write for the library, but I wasn't taking any material at that time, but he and I remained friends.

David Blocker produced many films with Alan Rudolph. I never knew where David found my name, but he called on me for help with many of his productions. One of them was *The Moderns*, which became a big film, and it had a few of our music selections in it. Another of his films was *Equinox* I think there were more than ten of our music selections in it, and it still shows on television. A couple of other films of his were, *Choose Me* and *Trouble in Mind*.

It was always good to get television shows, but somehow, getting in a feature film seemed more important when it came in. I never knew how big it would be, and, also, I never knew how far it would go into foreign markets, home video, and the Internet, all of which led to more income through those various avenues.

By 1986, I depended on word of mouth for my business. I didn't advertise, and I worked alone, but I could only do so much. I liked it and continued as long as I could. My work was so easy that I hated to tell anyone about it. My time was my own. I got many calls from first-time users letting me know that someone had recommended me. I always gave my best, and then most of those people came back again. Most editors went from one picture to another and knew where to get the best material. I worked with many of them, and they remained my most important clients.

32

You Are My Sunshine

Lucky Carle was probably my closest friend over the years, almost like a brother. We traveled together, played golf, and he, Jackie, and their daughter, Laura, were at my house almost every weekend for my Sunday barbecues. Somebody new joined us nearly every week at those barbecues, and there were sometimes more than thirty people using the pool, eating my food, and drinking Bloody Marys. I didn't mind doing the cooking and paying for it all. I never asked anyone for anything.

One Saturday, Lucky and I were playing in a foursome at Encino Golf Course. We said goodbye at the bar, and I drove Lucky to my house, as usual. I turned the corner and saw that there were many cars on the street. I said to him that someone must be having a party. I parked the car, and

Lucky Carle, Gloria, Roy

Roy, Gloria, Donovan and Linda

suddenly people burst from my house from all sides. They were there for my birthday, and I was completely surprised. I had never wanted anyone to that for me, but Gloria had put the party together and I knew nothing about it.

Lucky had been unhappy because he couldn't find work. He had left United Artist a year or two before, and nothing had turned up. I had tried with many people to hire him, but no one cared. He had made many hits happen for many artists and made a lot of money for people, but, as the saying goes, "What can you do for me now?" There were a few in high places that could have done something. I asked everyone, but there were no takers.

We were out on a golf course on a hot day, and Lucky became tired. He sat down on or about the fifteenth hole. I thought nothing more about it, but one night that week, I got a call from Jackie that they were taking Lucky to the hospital. The next call told me that he had passed away. His death was a complete shock. I think if he had been working he would have had more of a will to live, but he didn't want to be a burden on anyone. He was a proud man. I miss him to this day.

I must add that going into the office in the morning was not an easy thing at first. Setting the place up was no problem, but coming in and being alone was difficult. I decided I couldn't hire an assistant at the time because

I had no idea what I was in for. I would have liked to pay someone a nice salary, but at the time, that wasn't on my mind. Most of my business was done over the phone, or through an appointment made for someone to come in and listen to the music. License applications were still coming in from all over the country, and I handled the licensing and billing myself.

I opened an account at the Bank of Hollywood, which I called "my bank" because I was able to buy a lot of stock in the bank before it opened, thanks to a contact I had at the The Hungry Tiger Bar. It was the right bank for me because I knew everyone. If I needed extra money, I could go there and get it easily, but I never needed a loan. The bank was in our former Max Factor Building and easily accessible.

I had enough money to loan myself to buy recording equipment and build a good sound setup that would make good copies for my clients. Over the years, I kept up with the latest and always turn out copies on two reel to reel Technics 1500 tape recorders that worked well with clients. I also had a complete TEAC rack of equipment, and then at later dates, I added a powerful Sony amplifier to handle all inputs such as a DAT tape machine, which was important at the time, and a CD burner, which soon took over.

Even as late as 2000, I made my own copies and made sure the product that left the office was perfect for the client. Maybe that was why I worked alone; I was too much of a perfectionist. I only got one chance,

Roy, Gloria, Guy and Jackie Mitchell

and I didn't ever want to lose that chance. I had enough business to keep me busy and enough to back me up.

I had a great mechanic working on my cars, Bert at Bert's Garage on the corner of Selma and Cherokee in Hollywood. He kept my cars running good. I had been looking for a car for Gloria, and one day he showed me a Buick Coup. It looked great because it was a leased car from Max Factor. The girl who had been using it was getting another, and he said I should take it for Gloria. I did, and the car ran great for some time. We decided on a personalized license plate for it. In remembrance of the nickname Lucky called Gloria, we used "DeGonch."

33

Mama

On the evening of June 9, 1985, I got a call from my mom. She had just returned from Las Vegas with her group of senior citizens. She said she won and had a great time, which I knew meant that she had come home with what she started with. She went to bed, and either she must have been sick, or she somehow knew that something was wrong that night, because she pulled the clock out at 1:15 a.m. on June 10, the date of her wedding anniversary. She wanted to be with her departed husband, Frank. Mom never got up again.

A few days later, the coroner released her body, so she didn't get there by June 10. Al and I took her remains in a heavy casket to New York to be buried with Frank. Just as they were putting her in the ground, clouds opened to thunder, lightning, and rain. One of my cousins yelled out, "That's Frank yelling 'I thought I got rid of her.'" We all broke up and a good laugh was had by all twenty-five of my cousins, a fitting farewell for her.

Mom lived to be eighty-six, and she was a strong woman until the day she died. If we ever called her to say that we were coming over with a guest or two, she had a hot dinner ready and waiting on the table without ever having to go out and pick anything up.

I remember that when Al and I lived at home, we had a hot meal every night. Our mom loved to cook. She never worked, because in those days, many women were housewives after they married. I didn't realize she only cooked a few dishes because they always seemed different. Al and I had to eat fast to keep up with our father. I remember when she made Latkes (potato pancakes), they were very greasy, but we finished them off as soon as she put them on the table, and she couldn't keep up because they were so good, grease and all. I wish I could get some today that taste like those.

Bernie Brody and Mary Williams were the first two to operate a music clearing house and the first to call me, but over the years, many more followed. Mary was the head of Music Clearance at NBC. I met her first when I came out to California on one of my trips and hit it off with her right away. She confided with me about the move, and if I thought it was a good idea.

When Mary left NBC to open her own clearing house, Pete Lunn took over, and then came Martha Hanrahan. CBS had Donna Gunner, and starting there with her was Mary Kay Place. She went on to star in, *Mary Hartman, Mary Hartman*, and then many feature films. She was from Oklahoma, and I guess was lucky or happy to be with CBS.

Over the years, clearance houses became quite important. The major ones besides Mary William' were Fricon Entertainment Co. run by Terri Fricon. I actually met her when I went to a wine tasting. I became a member of the Bordeaux Sister City Affiliation. Los Angeles and Bordeaux, France were sister cities. Not bad when all the affairs featured wine tasting, and the best wines. The affairs were on the top floor of City Hall in Los Angeles. With Terri, at her company, were many assistants. Some were to go on and open their own clearance houses, including John McCullough, David Sibley, Gay Fusco, and others.

Clearance House Ltd. was run by Ron Gertz. Many of their personnel were to go to other places. Edwina Travis-Chin went to APM, one of my competitors, and the company Ralph tentatively set up for me to go to. Lynn Weisman, Kathy Anderson, and Suzi Barry went with Evan Greenspan, Inc., and Arlene Fishbach also opened her own business. Diane Prentice was with Mary Williams, but opened her own clearing house. Clearing houses did more than just clear films and television shows; they sometimes worked with the producers as consultants and music supervisors, and they helped in supplying source music. They all called me over the years, and we remained friendly. Other clearing houses were run by Steven Winogradsky, and there was one by Barbara Brunow.

When I dealt with any of those companies, I was sure to have correct cue sheets. The major part of their business was to get rates from publishers, publisher's information, and put it all together so there was no problem for producers at a later date. I found those people honest and helpful.

34

Almost Paradise

From 1985, when I went on my own, there was a definite pick up in business. I don't think it was going on my own, but just the times. It seemed that almost all television and feature film productions were starting to use more and more library music, and an unbelievable amount of features came in, small films and big releases. As an after thought, music editors find that they need something in a spot in the film where nothing had been composed.

I had listed a lot of early films, but the list grew to hundreds of big and small films that had anywhere from one song selection to many. Usually, the license is a buyout, and that meant the clearance was for all media, including television, Pay TV, videocassette, disc, theatrical, DVD, and anything that came along. The reason was that the clearance must cover all, as no one wanted a piece of music holding out for more money and holding a picture hostage. I tried to be congenial with all of my clients, and usually succeeded in being helpful in every way with the music and the money.

I was at a California Copyright Conference meeting one night, and on the dais was Ken Topolsky, a producer and director on many films and successful television series. He came over to say hello and proceeded to tell those around me that I was the most helpful person to him when it came to supplying music. He said that almost every time he called, I had what he needed, and I saved him a lot of time.

John McCullough began his own company, and he soon started to call me right away. Ken Topolsky soon produced, among others, *Party of Five*, and started to use the library often. John was the music consultant on the series.

From The Clearing Houses came many good features such as *Stealing Home, Little Man Tate,* and *Dead Before Dawn,"* and a few series such as *Probe, Lewis And Clark, The Bill Cosby Show,* and *Quit It*. Over the years The Clearing House was a major client.

Fricon Entertainment also called often. When John McCullough was there before he went into his own business, he called quite a few times with uses on *Cagney and Lacy*. Gay Jones (Fusco) called many times for many projects. One was a series called *The Days And Nights Of Molly Dodd*.

In 1987, John McCullough left Fricon Entertainment and opened his own business. He became a music consultant and started to pick up some television shows and series. He had Tony Scudellari with him. His first series was *Tour of Duty*. However, it was a short run. Also at the same time, he had a major series that ran a few years called *The Wonder Years*.

John's next was *Northern Exposure*. It seemed that our music selections were on almost every show. They had a juke box in the restaurant that played some great music, and I supplied a lot of that music. Martin Bruestle was the producer, but he was very involved with the music. He later moved on to *The Sopranos*.

John's next series was *Party of Five*, and I helped place music selections on almost every show. One of the producers I mentioned earlier was Ken Topolsky. All the above shows had long runs and were important to the library.

There was a show on HBO called *Not Necessarily The News*. It was Nancy Severinsen (Doc's daughter) who was the Music Supervisor. She was good at what she did, and music selections from our library were on quite a few of those shows.

In Mary Williams' office, while Diane Prentice was still there, they had an important series called *Mama's Family*, and music selections from our library was used often on the shows.

Stephan J. Cannell Productions also had quite a few series on. Michael Babcock was the Music Consultant for the shows. He also called me quite often. His office was on the next block from me, so I guess he liked the fast service. Our library was well represented on *Wise Guy, 21 Jump Street,* and *Hunter.* Michael moved on to work for another production library. Other Cannell shows using the library were *The Commish* and *Unsub*.

You may or may not sit and watch the credits at the end of a film or television show, but that is where you will find the name of the Music Supervisor or Music Consultant listed. They are the people who called me at the Southern Library for the music they need for a particular spot in a production. They knew what the budget for the music was, followed closely, and filled the spot within the budget. Then, if the music I sent fit the spot and definitely stayed in the production, they either sent me a license to sign or asked me to send my license, the fee asked, the license agreement of the different uses requested, such as theatrical, television film, non-theatrical, home video/disc(CD), and the territory and publisher involved. Then, also listed on theatrical film releases usually at the end of all the credits is a list of selections used, sometimes including the publisher, title, artist, and record company. Some of the supervisors or consultants with whom I worked were John McCullough, Evan Greenspan, Ron Gertz, Arlene Fishbach, Diane Wessel, Gary Callamar, Thomas Gollubic, Bonnie Greenberg, Dawn Soler, Celest Ray, Gregory Sill, and many more.

I often went to a theater and saw a good movie, and then I and a few others in the audience watched the end credits crawl by with the information about the people who made the film and where the film was made. Most of all, we heard all the great soundtrack music. People who left before the end credits missed a lot.

35

You're Nobody 'Til Somebody Loves You

In April 1986, Gloria and I decided to set May 2 as the date for our wedding. Ours was probably the longest engagement ever. We made calls, but nobody believed us. Gloria was Catholic, and I was Jewish, but not very religious. I decided to let her do her thing.

Fifteen people came to our wedding at St. Mel's in Woodland Hills. That was where she went to church and was a fitting place for our wedding. Gloria's family came and stayed at my house. Gloria's sister, Pat, came from Chicago. Her brother, Frank, and daughter, Kim, came. Cousin Beverly D'Andrea came, and from Palm Springs came her cousins Vince Pastere, and Larry and Marian Jarecki. Mort was my Best Man, and Gloria's brother, Frank, gave her away.

Just before we walked down the aisle, Monsignor Naughton said, "Now have a good time and no mistakes are ever made at weddings." I was waiting off to the side, when in came Frank and Gloria. Mort was at the altar with Gloria's sister, Pat, who was Maid of Honor. Frank and Gloria arrived at the altar and the ceremony began, but Monsignor Naughton mistakenly began to marry Gloria to Frank. Mort touched the Monsignor and pointed to me standing over to the side. We were brought correctly together, and the ceremony went right from then on.

I had met Monsignor Naughton a few times and he knew I wasn't Catholic. We talked about golf and the strange fact that he went to a Seminary in the East Bronx, where my mother's father once owned property on which the Seminary was located. However, they lost it during the 1929 market crash. Once again, it was a small world.

After the wedding, we met for cocktails at the home of my neighbors, Vic and Mimi Metzgar, and then we went to Musso & Frank's restaurant, perhaps the first time a wedding reception was ever held there. Owner Jesse donated all the champagne, which I did not know until the bill arrived later. Herb Alpert supplied us with a limousine that was supposed to be his own, one that Gloria had won in a raffle at one of the A&M picnics). There were fifteen of us and a cake big enough for 150 people. All the waiters were invited to have a slice. Everyone was able to order anything on the menu, and we had Sergio, the best waiter in town, serve us.

Bob Saget, who was in my nephew's amateur film back in high school, finally had a popular television show of his own, *America's Funniest Home Videos*. The show began broadcasting just before our wedding, and Gloria's cousin, Marian, from Palm Springs, got the bright idea to send the video that was taken by Larry, her husband. I didn't want to call Bob Saget or my nephew Bob, but I sent in the tape. Soon, I received a call that they wanted it, and then a letter including a release that had to be signed by everyone on the tape arrived. I wrote to those in Chicago and Palm Springs for their signatures, but it took too long to get them back. The show's producers started to get all those phony set up tapes, and ours got left out in the cold. We could have won. It was really funny seeing Gloria about to be married to her brother. However, I did sign a paper that I couldn't send it to any other show. I have a couple of lawyers in the family, Bob and Matt, and maybe we can still use it somewhere.

In July, we decided to have the real reception, a big party. I got tents and used my huge backyard. Brian Metzgar was a balloon man and he really did a job. My bartender was from Musso's. Reuben was the best. I invited most of the waiters, friends, some business associates, and of course, family members. We had close to 150 people. I had a small band, who I had helped in the office with many favors. He was Mexican and played all types of music, but it seemed it all had a Latin flavor. He came to me and said that the people wanted more music, and he asked if he should keep going for another hour. Of course, I say okay. When he came to get paid at the end, he charged me another couple of hundred dollars for that hour. He then stayed and had a good time, and to top it all off, he threw Gloria in the pool, ruining her dress and her evening. I did not see it, but everyone was quite mad. People stayed late and a great time was had by all.

1985 thru 1990 were the best years for our library. As a songplugger, it was important for me to bring income in through performances, and in my later years, whatever came in, I owned. During the late 1980s, there were a lot of important shows that increased ASCAP performance fees. *Small Wonder* ran for a few years and then went into syndication. Also, *Life Goes On* used my music quite heavily and the ASCAP earnings from that were quite good. Also, there was a mini series on PBS (but actually syndicated) called *Cosmos*, four two-hour shows, and that was shown many times. Those shows were re-edited from thirteen original 1980 episodes. Later, they re-edited them down to a two-hour production called *Best Of Cosmos*. Those Carl Sagan shows were extremely well-received and had longevity.

In 1990, I got a call from Terri Fricon asking if I had some Black Gospel music that could be used in *The Court Martial of Jackie Robinson*. I remembered that I had once entered into a deal with AVI through Ray Harris, where I could use some of his productions. He had recorded many Gospel albums. Ray told me it was all clear to use, but I had nothing in writing. I supplied a song selection called "Jesus Loves Me." The fee I quoted was in line with other uses in the film. After the film showed on television, I got a call from Terri about a letter from AFTRA concerning the singers. They wanted to be paid for their performance. I got a copy of the letter and told her I would take care of it. Ray Harris had since left AVI, so I was left hanging. I called AFTRA and spoke to someone, and told him the story about my deal with AVI, that Ray had left, and that I had nothing in writing. I had since sent AVI their royalty. I reached an agreement for $750. That was one production that cost me to get into, and I didn't even own the publishing, therefore there were no performances to help offset the loss.

36

Winchester Cathedral

Soon, I received notice that I was to be losing the Selected Sound Library. When I took over the library, it was owned by Peter Majewski. I met with him in New York, and he told me his son wasn't interested in it, and he was forced to sell it. Peter had since sold it to EMI in Germany.

I had been to Europe a few times. In 1990, I decided to make a business trip to meet with EMI and Famira, and I also wanted to take Gloria. I put together a good trip that began in Hamburg.

We landed in Hamburg, where Jan Famira picked us up and drove us to our hotel, the Atlantic Kempinski, a hotel that all the foreign dignitaries used. It was beautiful, and we had a room overlooking the lake. We had dinner and Jan was a good host. He had been very happy with our results with the Stereo Tape AG library.

After dinner, Jan dropped us off at the hotel and we decided to have a nightcap at a place overlooking the lake. We ordered a Martini, but in Germany, a Martini is just Martini and Rossi vermouth. We learned as we went along. In Germany, you drink beer. We got to the room at about 10:00 p.m. and the sun was still shining. It didn't get dark until around 11:30.

The next morning, I called Hans Muller of EMI Germany. We went to the office and it was good to meet the people with whom I corresponded. Hans told me of the decision of EMI taking all the libraries and putting them in one house. I could understand that. It was to take effect in December 1992. The Selected Sound Library had been a big money maker for the Southern Library of Recorded Music. That split led to bigger and better things).

We walked around town, and we had an appointment to stop off at a jewelry store that was owned by Jan Famira. In the back room, he had a small studio for making tape copies. All Gloria could see was a pile of diamonds on the table. After we left, she said, "Why didn't you ask him for a few?" I told him we were going to Zurich next. He told me what train to take, but he was wrong. I wanted to go past the Remagen Bridge, but the train we went on went another way.

Our first class Eurorail pass cost $315 each and could be used six times in a three week period. However, that leg of the trip was uneventful except for breakfast. There was a big heavy waitress, (I called her Brunhilde), who didn't speak English. I couldn't speak German when ordering basic eggs and other commonplace items, so I gave up and pointed to something. She delivered a big plate of lunch meat, cheese, and bread. We were the only ones in the dinning car on that wrong train.

Switzerland was beautiful with the scenic mountains and lakes. We arrived in Zurich and went to our hotel. Reservations had been made by Suzanne Klee's sister, who worked for Japan Airlines. We called Suzanne, who was the wild singer from Switzerland that once recorded in the United States, and then married and divorced. She told us that she would be at a county fair, or something like that, where she had a booth and was pushing a record. There was a show, and then we went out to eat with some of her friends. It was good to see her again. The people at the table all spoke English, I guess for our benefit. We had a lot of laughs, and it was a great evening.

We continued to tour through Zurich, Milan, Lake Lugano, Venice, Florence, and Rome, where we saw the Vatican and as much of Rome as we could see in four days there. We took the sleeper train to our office in Paris, and then from there, we took a train, having a great Sunday dinner in a beautiful dining car, to our office in Amsterdam, where we stayed at a great hotel. Peter Van Epen, Manager of the Amsterdam office, was a great host.

We flew to London, and we stayed at an expensive hotel on the top floor with a fire escape that was blocked with boxes. Gloria pointed out that no one could get out if they had to. They gave us a beautiful suite on the second floor at the same price, but still too much. We were on the wrong side of town. We wanted to be in Soho, where my office was. The hotel had a "guest sign-in book," and just before we were there, actress Sheryl Ladd was in that room and signed in. It was raining, but we found another hotel where we wanted to be. We met everyone at the Southern UK office and they were very nice to us.

The trip home was uneventful except for a seating mix-up, but we got back to Los Angeles. When I added it all up after all the credit card charges came in, the nineteen days cost $13,000.

At the end of 1991, we decide on getting a new car to replace Gloria's boring Buick, and we decided on a special order T-Bird with a sun roof. By the time it came in, it was a 1992 model. It ran great. We sold the Buick to Sergio, my waiter at Musso and Franks, and he ran it a long time after.

In 1993, I got a call from a Ken Wallace from ZM Productions. They needed a lot of music for a new half-hour show going on television that was to be called *Martha Stewart Living*. They picked a lot of music and he told me that she had to hear it before it could be used. That was my first experience with her, but I knew my work, and all the selections I picked were on the shows. Selections from the Southern Library were heard on the first fifteen shows she produced. I saw the shows and they came out pretty good. My music choices worked. However, I never did any more for them. I guess it was picked up by Universal and they did the rest.

I soon got a call that Southern Library LTD was to sell the United Kingdom copyrights to Zomba. They were to be released in the Brutan Library. With Ralph's help, I was able to keep all the USA copyrights until I was ready to retire. I went through all the titles and made a long list of the US copyrights that included the important Bluegrass and Country music. Zomba became a part of EMI in London, and I lost nearly everything to them. I soon worked a deal where they could release some USA selections, which helped my writers worldwide because Brutan was one of the largest libraries.

Also in 1993, Jon Caper and Doug Lackey were producing *Diana, Her True Story*, a major documentary that ran four hours and ran many times. I had quite a few pieces in it. I believe that was the most-shown documentary on Princess Diana.

Knowing a year before the Selected Sound Library would leave was a good thing. I was able to make some moves. Fred and Andy Jacobs of The DeWolfe Library had always wanted me to represent them in Los Angeles. I had called them a few times for things they had that I needed and it always worked out fine. I called and told them if they were still interested I would be available to represent them. A deal was set. They gave me a good price for their CDs. In fact, it helped me stay in business. DeWolfe had a great library and released more music than any library around, much better than Selected Sound.

I had been doing productions with Doug Lackey, a film music editor. He was very good at it. He was in an office with John Caper, and his company was called Triton Music. John had done many important features and won all kinds of awards. They always called me for source music, and they were working on many television shows. In 1994, they were thinking of moving. He was looking for a big enough place to include me. I told him I wanted to leave the 6777 Hollywood Boulevard building. They called me and we looked at some places. They came up with a house that was used as an office and wanted to know if I wanted to buy it with them. I said no, but I would rent. I did not want to be tied down with a few owners and have trouble when I was ready to quit.

They took the house, and I moved into two rooms, one for my studio and one for my office. It worked out fine, and was just about the same rent I paid in the old building. The house was on Cahuenga in Toluca Lake, right off the freeway. It took me twelve minutes to drive in. Don Vincent (who was building a recording studio in the garage), was one of the owners of the house along with John Caper and Doug Lackey. Mark Vincent, Don's son, was the engineer and ran the recording studio. At one time, Don was the orchestra conductor for Wayne Newton in Las Vegas.

NBC Productions had been calling about many of their shows, such as *Fresh Prince of Bel Air,* and Showtime was completing a major film called *Roswell.* They both used a few cuts. It seemed there was a call every day for music for one production or another. I found myself getting very busy turning out material. John McCullough was also getting very busy, and seemed to call me for everything.

Suzan Kapner (Mann) who worked for me at Peer Music became a Music Consultant. She called me for some Greek music for *Frankie and Johnny.* A film called *Roadside Prophet* needed some opera music and other selections. One after the other, they came in, including *Row Of Crows, Cadence, Drop Dead Fred, Too Much Sun, Little Man Tate, Swing Kids,* and many more.

37

Born To Lose

Gloria had been with Irving/Almo Music for twenty years. She, along with Margo Matthews and Pat Scoggins, had been the backbone of all copyrights going out to Washington. Gloria's signature was probably on 90-95 percent of the copyright papers. She had been on a first name basis with people in Washington, and had received accolades for the filing of those papers without errors for all those years.

Beginning in late 1992, they were starting to cut down staff at Irving/Almo. The first to go was Pat Scoggins, who was over fifty years old. Then, Margo Matthews, who was also over fifty, went. Then, starting in late 1993, Gloria got interoffice memos about certain projects for which she answered that they were done, and new projects, which she said would soon be done. She was an excellent worker and very diligent at what she did, but she was also over fifty, and was next on the list to be put out to pasture.

I legally can't enter the terms of the agreement, but they tried to pull a few fast ones on her. The person who was behind that "firing" really must have hated her, and had a personal endeavor to get her out, even though her work was impeccable. No good reason could be found to release her, but her termination finally came in April 1994. Gloria went to sign up for unemployment benefits, but she learned that she could not draw unemployment because there was a letter stating that she had quit. Even the personnel at the unemployment office laughed and said that was impossible. A hearing was set. The person behind all that was to appear, but no one showed up, so Gloria was able to get her unemployment benefits. If I were to publish in this book the original draft sent to Gloria, you would burst out laughing for what they tried to do. None of her bosses knew what they tried to do, but they terminated employment for Margo, Pat, and Gloria. Matt, Al's middle son, handled all that for us. I wanted to take them to court, but he said it would take too long, be too expensive, and we could lose.

Everyone at Irving, Almo, Rondor, and A&M Records received a plaque and recognition for being at the company for twenty years. Gloria always regretted she never got that recognition for all the work she did for them.

38

You Belong To My Heart

In 1996, I bought my second used car. I had been looking for a late model Jaguar. I had been happy with the 1975 model, but it had taken a beating, yet always came back for more. I found a 1993 XJ6 that was white with tan leather, almost brand new, and still under warrantee. It had only 38,000 miles.

I had gone on another European trip with Father Emilio, a friend of Gloria, who was also close to Frank Sinatra and had gone to Sinatra's funeral. We landed in Milan, journeyed to Monte Carlo, Cannes, Nice and all the main stops on the way to Lourdes. Then, we went to Bordeaux, and then to a few more cities, and finally reached Paris, with stops in Tours, Reims, and Orleans. On a second trip with him, we went to Italy, including Venice, Piza, Florence, Rome, Pompeii, Capri, Sorrento, and some side trips, and we even had an audience with The Pope.

The late 1990s proved very uneventful, except I went for my checkup in 1998 with Dr. Salberg. I had always had a heart murmur since I was a kid, but he told me the problem had worsened. I made an appointment with Dr. M. Ehrich, a cardiologist. I found out my aorta valve was only one half centimeter, when it should have been three centimeters. It opened, but was so slow that by the time it closed, all the blood leaked back. He said it wasn't life threatening as yet, but I should consider doing the surgery while there was time. I had also learned the same time of my original checkup that I had a prostate problem, but we chose to take care of my heart first.

I had a choice of either the teacher or student, so I took Dr. Yokoyama, the teacher, who was a genius. In July, I went to St. Joseph's Hospital in Burbank, and I wasn't scared. After having a bullet go through me in World War II, simple surgery was "a piece of cake," according to the doctor.

After the surgery, I woke up in the recovery room and I didn't even know the surgery had been done. Then, I found out I need a pacemaker. Two days later, I went back under the knife and got a pacemaker implanted. I had a lot of guests during recovery, which I didn't want in the hospital. I wanted rest.

While I was in the hospital, Father Emilio came to see me because we had become good friends. He was in his eighties and ran around like he was fifty. On the same floor with me a few rooms down was Cardinal Mahoney, who was in for some tests. When I told Father Emilio that he was there, he went looking for the Cardinal, but the door to his room was closed. Every time the Cardinal came walking past my room, he always looked in on me.

My nephew, Teddy, picked me up and drove me home. I felt good, due to Dr. Yokoyama's experience, and I couldn't even see where he had operated on me. My new heart valve was made out of cow skin, and was supposed to last fifteen years.

As soon as I got strong enough, I went to my neurological doctor, Dr. Leff, who informed me that my prostate was quite large. Another test confirmed that I had cancer. He sent me to the office of Dr. Lewinsky, the father of the Intern. I didn't see him; he was in New York or somewhere with his daughter. His assistant sent me to do a bone MRI and a few other tests. He then suggested going in and having the seeds placed. I really felt very uncomfortable there. I called Dr. Leff and asked him if I could make a change. He couldn't understand why they had even given me a bone test. He recommended Dr. Ozahan, a female doctor in Encino, who had a big setup on Reseda Boulevard. I went in, met her, and I liked her attitude. I told her where I had gone and mentioned the seeds. She said they probably wouldn't have worked because the cancer had broken out of the prostate and all I would need was the straight radiation. So I set up the treatment schedule of forty-two straight days at 8:30 a.m. every day. My PSA lowered from 8 or 9 to 0.3, and I had a Gleason 7 (the cancer number). I had done a lot of reading on that because prostate cancer was the one disease that gets diagnosed differently from one doctor to another. So, I was soon completely rebuilt with all new parts, and I felt great.

I came back to work at my office fast, and I had actually missed my work because I like what I do. I hadn't missed too much. When I got back, I just picked up where I left off.

In July 1999, I was driving to my office and I heard some bad news on the radio that Guy Mitchell had died on July 1 of complications after surgery. He had been living in Las Vegas with his wife, Betty, and every time we went to Vegas we had dinner with them. He was such a happy person, and we had many laughs with him. He and Gloria got along great. I really missed him because we had such a great relationship.

39

Return To Me

In 2000, a big farewell party was set to take place in Father Emilio's home town, Bassano Di Grappa, Italy. He had secured tickets for a Passion Play in Oberamergau. It was performed every ten years and was considered a must see. We went all through Switzerland including Innsbruck and many other cities along the way, and we enjoyed plenty of time in Venice, which was close to Bassano Di Grappa. I also finally got back to Remagen. The trip started in Amsterdam, Brussels, and Brugges. The bus then took us to where we were to meet a river boat on the Rhine River about ten miles south of Remagen. I asked the bus driver and passengers if they would mind the side trip for a couple of hours. All said yes. In fact they asked me to tell my story, the same story that opens this book. The bus had a good microphone and speaker system, so it was easy to sit and just relate my story so everyone could hear.

I was so taken with the museum at the bridge that I screwed up all of it on my video camera, and had to get a copy from someone else on the trip. They all thanked me for the story and also the exceptional side trip. Most of the people on the trip had lived during World War II.

40

Sway

In 1998, my nephew, Bob, had an Internet company, www.goodnoise.com, which was a site from which people could download songs, the same as Napster, but he charged the downloader and paid publisher and record company royalties. I advanced him a few dollars, and the company soon went public. The name was changed to E-MUSIC. I soon got an envelope in the mail with a certificate for many shares in the company, something I didn't expect. He was then on the NASDAQ and did very well. It was an awful, uphill battle, and Napster was ruining the business giving away free music over the Internet. Meanwhile, stock for emusic.com went as high as $35 a share. I could only sell when I submitted a request in writing because they were called "restricted shares." However, I was able to sell some at $19 and $21, so I came out okay.

His business was moving slowly and becoming more difficult when others were giving music away free. In 2001, he was able to work out a deal with Universal Music Group to purchase the company. Universal probably had big plans for emusic.com, since the site was still on the Internet. Universal bought the rest of my shares for 50¢ each.

Bob continued his genius efforts by creating another Internet site at www.laugh.com, and the site did well offering free jokes and selling CDs of comedians. His main partner was George Carlin. Bob's brother, Ted, managed the shipping and other administrative details. Bob also started a new company called Royalty Share, a collection agency for revenues for music publishers, record companies and artists. On radio and television, there are performance royalties for publishers and writers, However, the Internet brought big changes in the way royalties were collected for all. Collection efforts for artists had been brought up in front of Congress many times, but with no definitive action.

Matthew, who was Al's middle son, and his wife, Sharon, were involved with a film called *The Basket* that won an award for the Best G-rated Film. *The Basket* was about a basketball kid's team in Seattle, and the film was well-done.

Al soon retired, and he and Edna had become great-grandparents, and they lived one block from me. Mort retired and married Nancy, an old friend, and he also lived a block away. Jackie continued to live in the apartment that she and Lucky lived in. Their daughter Laura got married and lived in Fallbrook, not too far from us.

Matt and Sharon lived in Santa Monica with their sons, Frankie and Samuel Leroy. Bob and Lori lived in Pebble Beach with their children, Katie and Joey. Ted and Joanne had Todd and Beth, now married to Alan, and had sons, Jordan and Jason.

Gloria and I had no children, so I became everyone's uncle. Gloria's sister, Pat, married to Al and had three children. Gina had two children, Ally and Jake. Bryan and Albert were single. Gloria's brother, Frank, had three children, Frank, Jr., Johnny, and Kim. Gloria had another brother, Bob, married to Emily. Gloria's mom, Phyllis, was still strong at the age of ninety-six, however she will pass away at 98 years old Christmas 2007.

41

Sugartime

In 2000, it was so great to see people move on to get other shows and still use my music. Martin Bruestle from *Northern Exposure* became a producer on *The Sopranos,* and he called me when he needed something. Along came *Six Feed Under*, another HBO show. I got a call from a Thomas Golubic. He and Gary Calamar were the Music Supervisors, and from the first piece of music I sent to them, they raved about my service and the music that they couldn't get anywhere else. My knowledge of Opera helped. Thomas recommended me to a few other people. My new business was still largely generated by word of mouth.

A television series strived to be successful long enough to produce 100 or more shows so that when the series ends, the show could go into syndication and rerun seemingly forever. I considered myself lucky to have many series in syndication so that earnings kept coming in through ASCAP, such shows as *Third Rock From The Sun, Party of Five ,Northern Exposure, Family Matters, Fresh Prince of Bel Air,* and *Archie Bunker,* among others.

Some companies continued putting people out to pasture before their time. In my opinion, an alert man or woman who did a good job at any age should not be fired. I'm sure that bosses could work something out and keep them on. That applied to me, too.

The Southern Library was a British Company that never opened in the United States until I took it over in 1985. Many of the copyrights were still in Southern Music Publishing Company, (ASCAP). Since I had back in the 1970s obtained Ralph's permission to open SLRM/Southern in ASCAP, the performance payments were directed to the right place after I moved most of the copyrights to the Southern Library. Some of the copyrights were still with Southern Music and they just weren't moved to the new firm. Only I knew about that setup. A film company cleared a piece of music with Southern Music, a library piece, but on paper it was SMP. I went through a lot of interoffice e-mails concerning those copyrights with my own SMP and I couldn't get to first base until the last e-mail got to Kathy Spanberger. She added at the end of all the other mail, "Roy Kohn has been with Southern for over forty years. If he says it's with SLRM/Southern, it's with SLRM/Southern."

I think every business needs senior citizens on the staff. If I had been able to put another like me on, I would have. I know there's always a concern with health insurance, but I think something can be worked out.

During 2001 and 2002, I knew I was coming to the end of my work in the music business. If I had it to do all over again, I would. I had a good time and made a lot of friends. I don't know what else I would have done, but that work suited me fine. The last two years were somewhat busy. I got calls, but not as many as before. Almost all my clients that have used my music still called, but I did not seek out new clients. I spent most of my time writing this book and just making copies of all my reel-to-reel tapes onto DAT, and then transferring the whole library onto CDs, a monumental job, but I enjoyed the work because I got to listen to all the music and learn more. I never forgot a melody. I knew I wouldn't be able to walk out and close the door behind me; I'm not that type. Jan Famira still basically owned the classical tapes, and the great DeWolfe Library would go back to Andy Jacobs. What was left of Southern Library copyrights would be taken over by Brutan (EMI).

Music publishing today has become very difficult. It has come around to the way it was 40 years ago. Just a handful of publishers. Many of the major publishers have merged with conglomerates and now there are not the amount of companies to contact. Sony, Warner Bros., EMI, NBC Universal and a handful of others are the only places to go. The company I'm still associated with, PEERMUSIC, is still the largest independent with branches all over the world. It is great because the standard catalogue keeps getting used.

The Supervisors and Music Consultants are the important contact for TV and Feature Films, and for the writer this of course is difficult unless you know them There are many lists around, and these people are easy to find. As I mentioned earlier just watch the credits at the end of a production and you will see the name.

My business now, a music library, has become a something else. Music Libraries now are companies like " Taxi" who carry hundreds of songs by different writers. They supply songs and artists to these producers, consultants and supervisors. I personally don't like this type of setup as you don't know if your material is being worked.

I believe the best way to get your material heard is find a group (band), make a good demo, and push the package.

Most of the major artists record there own material and also keep the complete package and getting a song in is not easy but it does happen.

Now the internet is another story. I wish I knew if places like You-Tube will ever become the main entity.

I have thought about retiring, but I had so much gusto left that I planned to do some traveling with Gloria to Europe again and to the east coast and revisit White's Clam Bake in Old Orchard Beach and the many other good restaurants I used to frequent.

42

The End?

On September 9, 2002, I played in the annual Pacific Pioneer Broadcasters golf tournament. The next day, I felt weak and had a stiff back and neck. I called Dr. Salberg and made an appointment then a colonoscopy. Results showed that I had colon cancer and needed to be immediately booked into Tarzana Hospital because he was worried about a blood infection I also had and it could effect my rebuilt aorta valve. Dr Morrow, my surgeon, postponed the colon surgery when a blood clot was found in my left leg. Another fast surgery cleared the clot, or I could have lost my leg. After that, the colon surgery was performed and I came out fine. There were post-surgery complications, but I survived.

I had survived a paralyzing bullet in World War Two, open heart surgery, prostate cancer, and colon cancer, and I was still around.

In 2004, while driving home after looking at new houses in the Palm Springs area, I had to urinate real bad and it was burning. The next day I saw my Dr.Leff and he put me in the hospital where after some tests they found I had a tumor in my bladder and it was cancer. That's cancer number three. The surgery was a success and Dr. Leff told me if I did not have another cancer by 2007 I would be cancer free.

In 2005, Gloria and I moved to that house in a new development (Tuscany) in Rancho Mirage Ca., where we would be near Gloria's relatives in case something again happened to me. Gloria was constantly with me during all the surgeries and even though it was rough for me, it must have been worse for her. She was told 3 different times to prepare for the worst.. She had many prayer groups around the country praying for me. Many people think that she is a healer.

Gloria and I do more here than we ever did before. We go to many shows, luncheons and dinners and we are kept busy. I have a Thursday luncheon every week with from 30 to 40 men who were all associated with show business. The stories, Jokes etc. make it feel like a little Friars Club. Steve Petersen, one of the Thursday group, had several conversations with Gloria and recognized her healing powers. He had written a book called HEALER.

April 2010 I picked up pneumonia on a cruise, however I booked another cruise for Oct.2010. A glutton for punishment, and I'm only 86.

I began all the chapters in this book with the title of a song that I was associated with or worked on. There is one song I worked on in the 1950s when I was with Joy Music that was written by Milton Berle and recorded by Arthur Godfrey, and the song sums up how I feel about life: "I'd Give a Million Tomorrows For Just One Yesterday."

Index

10,000 Bedrooms, 67
"1812 Overture", 59 , 156
21 Jump Street, 112
47th Regiment, 13

A&M Records, 116, 135, 184
AFRTS, 102, 131, 159
ASCAP, 40. 64, 81, 100, 114, 128
A Funny Thing Happened On The Way To the Forum, 67
A Gliss To Remember, 54
Academy Of Country Music, 124
Alamo, The, 73
"Amor", 76 , 81
"An Affair to Remember", 61
Ackers, Andy, 67
Adams, Chick, 17
Adams, Nancy, 108
Addy, Mickey, 17
"Ali Baba", 41`
Alhert Jr. Fred, 56
Allen, Fred, 6
Allen, Steve, 39, 64
Allen, Woody, 6
Alexander, Nick, 130
Alpert, Herb, 135
Alta Communications, 147
Ames, Ed, 29, 93
Alroy Music, 40
Ambrose & His Orchestra, 81

Amore, Ann, 147
Amsterdam, Morey, 18
Anderson, Kathy, 170
Anderson, Lynn, 97, 116,
Andrews, Julie, 55, 56
Andrews Sisters, 24
Anka, Andy, 64
Aquitania, 12, 15
"Atlantis", 99
"Arthur, You Should Smile More", 57
Artist Films AG, 82, 92
Atanasio, Pat, 85, 91
"Autumn Leaves", 55
AVI Records, 135, 139, 141
"Awful Weary", 41

BMI, 40, 181, 180
Baca, Miguel, 95, 97, 102, 105, 107, 129
Bacharach, Burt, 116
NBC Bandstand, 54
Barber, John, 115
Barclay Records, 41
Barclay Record Shop, 56
Barnes, George, 54
Barney Miller Show, 155
Barnum, H. B., 134
Barry, Red, 122
Barry, Suzi, 170
Barton, Eileen, 32
Basket, The 192

Bassano Di Grappa, 189
Bassey, Shirley, 128
Battle Beyond The Stars, 155
Baxter, Betty Jo, 76
"Be Mine Tonight", 89
Becker, Gene, 47, 48
Becker, Walter, 123
Bee, Celi, 147
Bell, Jerry, 135
Bennett, Tony, 82
Berle, Milton, 50, 64
Berlin, Irving, 48
Berkowitz, Howard, 127, 129
Bernard, Bobby, 59
Bernhart, Milt, 39
Bernstein, Louis, 22
Benny, Jack, 6, 17, 20, 71
Berry, Dennis, 85, 92, 99, 133, 141
"Besame Mucho", 89
"Big Mamou", 134
Big Band Night, 139
Big Three, The, 56, 64. 85, 91
Billboard Magazine, 40
Biondi, Dick, 78, 88
Birch, Jack, 62
Black, Ted, 64, 77, 92

Blanch, Arthur, 155
Blazing Stewardesses, 122
Blever, Archie, 43
Block, Gene, 51, 60. 102, 111
Block, Martin, 9, 50, 51, 62
Block, Shirley, 61, 148
Blocker, David, 162
"Blue Moon Of Kentucky", 155
Blue Yodel, 80
Bonanza, 63
Boone, Pat, 60
Borchetta, Mike, 112
"Born To Lose, 76
"Brazil", 134
"Breakfast Club, 88, 89

Breedlove, Jimmy, 53
Bridgewater, Leslie, 85
Bright Promise, 114
Brill, Richard, 153
Brill Bldg. (1619 Bway.), 29 , 81
Brooks, Mel, 35, 36
Brody, Bernie, 171
Brotz, Elliott, 6
Bruestle, Martin, 193
Brunow, Barbara, 170
Brown, Larry, 32
Bryant, Anita, 45
Bunker, Archie, 157, 193
Burdoff, Dorothy, 36
Buzzell, Loring, 24

Cadence Records, 43, 44
California Copyright Conference, 115, 145, 171
Callamar, Gary, 173
Camp Edwards Convalescent Hospital, 16
"Can't You Hear My Heart Beat" 81, 112
Caper, John, 181
Captain and Tennille, 135
Carle, Frankie, 27, 33
Carle, Jackie, 77, 107, 108, 113, 165
Carle, Lucky, 33, 38. 67, 68, 75, 77, 107. 108, 113, 121, 128, 130, 165, 166
Carlin, George, 191
Carlone, Laura, 113, 165, 192
Carnival, 73
Carpenters, The, 135
Carr, Vikki, 135
Carroll, Jimmy, 57
Carroll, June, 35
Carson, Johnny, 87
Carson, Mindy, 32
Carter, Ray, 57
Carter Family, The, 80
Cash, Johnny, 77
"Catch The Wind", 41, 147
Carter And Lewis, 112

Index

Champagne For Breakfast, 143
Chapman, Ben, 6
Charles, Ray, 75, 76
Charles (Singers), Ray, 81, 87, 88
Charlie Chaplin Studios, The 135
Checchi, Dottie, 23, 41
Chordettes, The, 45
Choose Me, 112
Clark, Dick, 32
Clark, Sam, 43, 44
Clarke, Buddy, 20
Clary, Robert, 35
Clarckson, Art, 97
Claws, 128
Clayton, Bob, 23, 41, 77
Clearing House, 170
Coe, Frank, 116, , 141
Cohen, Paul, 50
Collins, Lester, 75
Columbia Pictures, 18
Commish, The, 172
"Confess", 27
"Coo Coo Roo Coo Coo, Paloma", 104
Conti, Mario, 83, 85, 91, 113, 153
Cooke, Victoria, 155
Cooper, Pat, 49
Como, Perry, 88
Corelli, Franco, 59, 74, 75
Corelli Jacobs, 82, 100, 151
Country Music Association, 124
Cosby, Bill, 171
Court Marshall of Jackie Robinson, The, 177
Craig, George, 151
Craig, Teresa, 151
Crane, Bob, 19, 102
Creston Junior High School, 6, 8
Creston Music, 40, 59'120
Crestonians, The, 8
Crosby, Bing, 24, 46
Cross, Barbara, 148, 149
"Cumana", 13
Currie, Sherie, 152

Dallas, 157
Damone, Vic, 18, 29, 60
Davis, Donna, 149
Davies, Brian, 45, 60, 67, 119
Davis Jr., Sammy, 29
De Carlo, Yvonne, 122
De Grazia, Ted, 105
Dessau, 10
Darin, Bobby, 71, 76
Day, David, 65
Dead Before Dawn, 171
Deadly Nightshade, 138
"Deep In The Heart Of Texas", 77
"Deep Purple", 62
Delta Airlines, 138
Dempsey, Jack, 39, 76, 78
Dentzel, Carl, 105
Dern, Bruce, 115
DeWolfe Library, 194
DeWitt Clinton High School, 8, 9
Diamond, Morris, 21, 88
Diana, Her True Story, 181
Diante, Denny, 105, 107, 116, 117, 121, 130, 137
Dickinson, Angie, 116
Diesel, 155
Different Strokes, 157
DiMaggio, Joe, 6
Disneyland, 71
Disneyland Hotel, 144
Domino, Fats, 60
Donovan, 91, 160
"Don't Wait Too Long", 82
Dorado Beach Hotel, 68
Dorsey, Jimmy, 6, 24
Dorsey, Tommy, 6, 8, 24
Downey Jr., Morton (Sean), 50
Dr. Dracula, 155
Drive In, 139
Drop Dead Fred, 182
Dunk, Han, 88

Eckstine, Billy, 28
Eddy, Duane, 7
Dr. Ehrich, 183
E-MUSIC, 191
Embassy Pictures, 121
Epen, Peter Van, 180
El Norte, 161
Equinox, 162
Erpel, 13
Essex Films, 141
Fagen, Donald, 123
Faktor, Jeri, 144
Fallon (Welk), Tanya, 96
Family Matters, 103
Famira, Jan, 92, 128, 135, 179
Farley Mike, 88
Farrow, Johnny, 27, 34, 107
"Fascination", 55
Father Emilio, 185, 189
Feist, Leo, 1, 56
Feller, Sherm, 38
Ferrante and Teicher, 137
Fiedler, Arthur, 23
Filmation, 121
Final Countdown, 151
Fine, Bob, 35
Fishback, Arlene, 170, 173
Fisher, Eddie, 29
Flast, Barry, 152
Flatto, Jerry, 42
Fleischmann, Mort, 29, 55. 56, 79, 85, 93, 97, 135
Flynn, Errol, 64
Folk, Robert, 162
Foley, Norm, 56, 65, 73
Ford, Lita, 152
Ford, Milton Q., 33
"Forever", 47
Forsythe, John, 97
Fowley, Kim, 125
Frances, Connie, 44
Frankie and Johnny, 182

Freed, Allen, 54
"Frenesi", 141
Fresh Prince Of Bel Air, 182, 193
Friar's Club, 35, 50
Friedlander, Buddy, 24, 29
Fricon, Terri, 170, 172, 177
"Friendly Persuasion", 60
From Cassino To Korea, 155
"Funny How Love Can Be", 112
Fusco, Gay, 170

Gallaher, Ed, 33
Gar, Larry, 77
Garcia, Provie, 129
Garfunkel, Art, 151
Garrett, Patsy, 35, 104, 134
Gart, John, 64
Geary, Jeanne, 54
Gehrig, Lou, 6
Geller, Harvey, 40
"Georgia On My Mind", 75, 141, 151
Gershwin, George, 2
Gerstenfeld, Ken, 161
Gertz, Ron, 170, 173
Gibson, Don, 116
Gilda, 18, 20
Girls For Hire, 122
Glass, Mickey, 18
Gleason, Jackie, 62
Gloom Dodgers, 18
Golubic, Thomas, 173, 193
Godfrey, Arthur, 45, 62
Goncher, Gloria, 127, 131, 135, 136, 148, 154, 168, 175, 181, 183, 184, 192, 197
Ghostley, Alice, 34,
Gilley, Mickey, 133
Goodman, Benny, 6, 8, 24
Gorme, Edie, 39
"Granada", 76
Grandpa Jones, 21
Graham, Ronny, 35, 36

"Grande Grande Grande", 135
Greenberg, Bonnie, 173
Greenspan, Evan, 170, 173
"Greenleaves Of Summer, The", 73
Griffin, Merv, 64
Guarino, Bob, 116, 129
Guarnieri, Armond, 8
Guarnieri, Johnny, 46, 54, 57
Gunner, Donna, 170

Haggard, Merle, 147
Hale, Corky, 88
Haley, BIll & The Comets, 45
Halloran Hospital, 16
Hamburg Radio Symphony Orchestra, 82
Hamburg Symphony Orchestra, 82, 183
Hammell, Mrs., 9
Hamilton, Arthur, 120
Hanrahan, Martha, 170
Harris, Ray, 135, 139, 141, 152, 177
Haskell, Jimmie, 111, 117
Hawaii Production Center, 131`
Hawkins, Dolores, 24, 88
Hayman, Richard, 39
Hayworth, Rita, 18
Heatherton, Joey, 63
Herman's Hermits, 91
Hicklin, Ron, 109, 116
Higgins, Anita, 138
Hilda, 6
Hirsch, Roberta, 6
Hodges, Bob, 23
Holly, Buddy, 75, 128
Hook, Dr., 147
Hollywood Bowl, 97
Hopkins, Mary, 107
Horn, Bob, 32
Horton, Johnny, 73
Horton, Roy, 76, 125
Hotter, Dr. Charles, 138
"How Much Is That Doggie In The Window", 37, 56

Howe, Buddy, 31
Howe, Nancy, 31, 64
Huddleston, Floyd, 108
Hudson, Harvey, 33, 108
Hughes, Marjorie, 27
Hughes, Thom, 9
Humonoids From The Deep, 155
Hummert Radio Features, 17
Hungry Tiger, 116
"Hurdy Gurdy Man", 99

"I Can't Get You Out Of My Heart", 87
"I Love You A Thousand Ways", 147
The Incredible Two Headed Transplant, 115
"I'm A Fool To Care", 151
"In The Jailhouse Now", 77, 147
Independent International Pictures, 122
"I Overlooked An Orchid, 123
"It's Incredible", 115
Insetta, Paul, 36
Insight, 115
Almo, Irving, 135
"It's You Again", 147
"It Wasn't God Who Made Honky Tonk Angels", 116, 138
Iversen, Bob 75, 85

Jacobs, Andy, 157, 194
Jacobs, Fred, 151,
Jaxon, Bob, 41, 46, 53, 55
"Jennifer Juniper", 99
Jenkins, Gordon, 28
Jennings, Waylon, 125, 155
"Jesus Loves Me", 177
Jolson, Al, 21
Jolson Story, The, 20
Jones, Tom, 155
Jordan, Kappi, 31, 32
Joy, Eddie 27
Joy, George, 27, 28, 37, 40
Joy Music, 29, 71
Judas, Bernice, 24

Kallen, Kitty, 64
Kantor, Hy, 71
Kapner, Suzan, 130, 149, 152, 182
Kapp, Dave, 55
Kapp Records, 55, 96
Kapp, Mickey, 55
Kaye, Barry, 61, 96
Kaye, Stubby, 8
Kelly, Jack, 20
Kelly, Paula, 139
Kellerman, Sally, 116
Keyser, Kay, 24
Kingston, Bob, 114, 129, 130, 137
Kitt, Earth, 35, 73
Klaven, Jack, 33
Klee, Suzanne, 153, 154, 180
Klinger, Emily, 113
Knieste, Adam, 40
"Knock Knock Who's There", 107, 111, 113
Kohn, Al, 7, 31, 32, 56, 59, 114, 120, 192
Kohn, Bob, 120, 121, 191
Kohn, Edna, 56, 59, 114, 120, 102
Kohn, Matt & Sharon, 123, 192
Kohn, Teddy & Joanne, 183, 192
Krupa, Gene, 24
Kugler, Al, 95, 112

"La Boutique Fantastique", 59, 60
Lacy, Jack, 79
Ladelle, Jack, 46, 48, 54
Ladd, Cheryl 180
Lamond, Don, 46
Lackey, Doug, 152, 162, 131, 182
Landers, Bob, 63
Landon, Michael, 63
Lang, Edith, 85
Lanza, Edith, 50, 53
Lawrence, Steve, 29 35, 39, 64, 88
Laugh. com, 191
LaVine, Marilyn, 80
Lawrence, Carol, 35
Lazare, Paul, 82, 92

"Lazy River", 76
Lear, Norman, 137
Lee, Peggy, 8, 102
Leff, Dr., 186, 197
Leigh, Mitch, 111
Leonard, Jack E., 50
Lennon Sisters, 92
Leonetti, Tommy, 50
Lessberg, Jack, 54
Levy, Len, 130
Lewis, Bill, 59
Lewis, Jerry Lee, 91, 116
Lewis And Clark, 157, 171
Les Vegas & Bobby Woods, 53
Liberace, 135 148 153
Life Goes On, 176
"Limehouse Blues", 47, 48
"Little Bit O'Soul", 99, 112
Little Man Tate, 171
"Lonesome Whistle", 116
Los Indios Tabajaras, 82
Lost Horizon, 116
"Lost Little Child", 1
Loughery, Jackie, 36
"Love Me With All Your Heart", 81, 87, 151
Lowey, Jay, 71
Lucas, Buddy, 54
Lucraft, Howard, 114, 139
Lowe, Mundell, 46
Lowery, Bill, 33
Lunn, Pete, 170
Lyman, Abe, 17, 24
Lynde, Paul, 35

MacHarg, Eddie, 71
MacRae, Gordon, 2
"Mama's Tired", 54
Magid, Lee, 24
Magnus, Johnny, 63
Malbin, Elaine, 100
Manhattan Merry Go Round, 9, 17, 21
Malinou, Sherri, 88

Mamma's Family, 172
Mancini, Ginny, 139
Mancini, Henry, 102
Mann, Herbie, 155, 159
Manning, Bob, 41
Mantle, Mickey, 5
Elena, Maria (Buddy Holly), 68
Elena, Maria, 82
Maris, Roger, 6
Mary Hartman, Mary Hartman, 137. 138, 145, 138, 151, 156
Marks, Edward B., 1
Martino, Al, 35, 87
Martin, Dean, 18
Martin, Tony, 18
Marshall, Jerry, 23, 73
McCullough, John, 170, 171, 172, 173
McGuire Sisters, 45
"Mas Que Nada", 91
Mathis, Johnny, 60
Matthews, Eddie, 111, 112, 135
Matthews, Margo, 127, 183
"Maybe I'll Cry Over You", 155
McCune, Bill, 21
McDevit, Barney, 71
McKinley, Verne, 13, 14
McKinnley, Ray, 13, 14
McLean, Don, 76, 155
McMaster, Jay, 93
Meath, Ed & Joe Deane, 78
Majewski, Peter, 128
Mendez, Sergio, 91,
"Mellow Yellow", 91, 159
Merrill, Bob, 28, 32, 36, 37, 56, 73, 102
Metropolitan Opera, 74
Miller, Glenn, 6, 7, 24
Miller, Glenn Orchestra, 57
Miller, Jodi, 16
Miller, Mitch, 27, 36
Miller, Warren Productions, 152
Mills, Marty, 29
Mink, Alan, 79

"Miss You Babe", 144
Mitchell, Guy, 28, 36, 37, 186, 187
Mitchell, Keith, 121, 122
Moderns, The 162
Moffo, Anna, 74
Mogull, Ivan, 10
Moline, Bob, 153
Montalban, Ricardo, 117
Mood music, 17, 18, 25
Morgan, Jane, 55
Moore, Garry, 88
Morrow, Dr., 197
"Moten Swing", 141
"Movin' Along", 57
Murray The "K", 56
Mostel, Zero, 67
"The Music Goes Round And Round", 8
Music Sound Track Service, 82, 100
Muller, Hans, 179
Musso And Frank, 142
"My Foolish Heart", 28
"My Heart cries For You", 28
"My Truly, Truly Fair", 28

Napster, 191
NASDAQ, 191
Naughty Stewardesses, 122
Nelson, Willie, 125, 138, 147, 157
"Never Never Never", 128, 136
New Faces of 1952, 35
New Music Co., 151
Newjack Sound, 116
Newman, Bob, 115
Newman, Jack, 79, 82
Newman, Roger, 79
New Marketts, 138
Nilsson, Brigit, 74
Ninth Division, 12
"Nocturne For Lovers", 114
North Dallas Forty, 151
Northern Exposure, 172, 193
Not For Women Only, 133, 151

"North To Alaska", 67
Nuriev, Rudolf, 60

O'Brian, Angie, 148
Obsession, 128
O'Connell, Helen, 24, 139
Old Orchard Beach, 76
Orlando, Tony, 77
Osborne Brothers, 155
Ovens, Don, 73
Overwise, Mickey, 64
Oxford Music, 25

P.S. 79, 5, 9
Pacific Pioneer Broadcasters, 104
Page, Kathy, 1, 31, 33, 71
Page, Patti, 1, 27, 37, 71
Pansullo, Betty Jo, 108
Pansullo, Jim, 23, 108
Paramount Records, 111
Paramount Theater, 7
Party Of Five, 171, 172, 193
Parish, Mitchell, 61
Passion Play, The/Oberammergau, 189
"Patricia", 77
Payolas, 20
Pease, James, 153
Peatman List, 20, 68
Peer, Elizabeth, 113
Peer, Elizabeth Ann, 113
Peer, Mary Megan, 11
Peer, Monique, 75, 80, 82, 93, 95, 108, 122, 129, 145
Peer, Ralph, 80, 82, 108, 143
Peer, Ralph, 11, 80, 85, 73, 94, 95, 102, 107, 113, 114, 149, 159, 162
Peer, Ralph, 111 113
Peer International Music, 81, 107
Penney, Ed, 23
Peter And The Wolf, 153
Petersen, Charlie, 45, 93, 130
Petersen, John, 89

Peterson, Steve, 198
Pierce, Capt., 15
Pierno, Christina, 91, 95
Pincus, George, 17
"Pipsqueak Parade", 54
"Pittsburg Pennsylvania", 28
Police Academy, 2
Police Academy 7, 162
Powell, Gay, 148
Powell, Teddy, 53
Prado, Perez, 77
"Premiere Occaision", 137, 138
Prentice, Diane, 170
Prescott, Michael, 120
Prescott, Norm, 23, 24, 41, 120
Prima, Louis, 29, 88
Prima, Tracy, 88
The Probe, 171
Pryor, Richard, 124

Quit It, 171

"Race The Sun", 134, 151
Rael, Jack, 27, 31, 36, 37
Ramone, Phil, 45
Ranch, Harry, 21
Rancho Mirage, 21
Randall, Bill, 54
Ray, Celeste, 173
Rayburn, Gene, 39
Raye, Martha, 139
Rebidas, Lorraine, 31
Reisman, Joe, 31
Remagin Bridge, 12, 13, 139
Remmick, Jerome, 1
Repo Man, 157, 161
"Return To Me", 151
Revenge Of Agent X, 122
Reynolds, Debbie, 60
Richards, Stan, 23, 41
Richie Family, The, 134
Richland, Tony, 122

Ritz Brothers, The 122, 123
Roadside Prophet, 182
Robbins, Feist and Miller, 56, 120
Roberts, Art, 78, 89
Robessa, Jim, 39, 40
"Rock And Roll Yodel", 53
Rodriguez, Chill, 68
Rodgers, Jimmie, 80
Rollini, Adrian, 21
Rondo, Don, 53
Rooftop Singers, The, 82
Roswell, 182
"The Roving Kind", 28
Row Of Crows, 182
Runaways, The, 152
Rudolph, David, 162
Ruth, Babe, 6

Sagan, Carl, 177
Safranski, Eddie, 46
Saget, Bob, 120
Salberg, Dr., 197
Salinger, Manuel, 88
Sandy and Sally, 97
Sanacola, Frank, 29
Sanford and Son, 157
"Santa Baby", 36
Santly Joy, 25
Saracino, Joe, 138
"Sausalito Summer Night", 155, 159
Schindler, Catherine, 102, 105, 107, 129, 135, 140, 160
Schlesinger, Al, 130
Schoninger, Stu, 130
Schuster, Wally, 18
Scoggins, Pat, 183
Second Time Around, The, 67
Scopp, Mickey, 56, 64, 73
Scott, John, 134, 151
Scruggs, Earl, 155
Sears, Zenas, 33
Selected Sound, 128

Sex World, 142, 143
"Shackles and Chains", 151
Shannon, Harry, 154
Shapiro, Maurice, 2
Shapiro-Bernstein, 2, 8, 17, 20, 25, 32
Sharron, Marti, 136
Shaw, Artie, 24
Shawker, Bunny, 54
Shawnee Golf Club, 62
Sherman, Sam, 122
Sibley, David, 170
Sill, Gregory, 173
Simmons, Richard, 157
Simms, LuAnn, 25
Sinatra, Frank, 8, 24, 29, 76
"Since I Don't Have You", 76, 128, 151, 1565
Skelton, Red, 6
Skylar, Sunny, 75, 76
Slezack, Erika, 119
Sleeper, 130
Slanger, Frances Y., 15, 16
Small Wonder, 176
Smith, Joe, 25
Smith, Kate, 29
Smith, Keely, 29
Soler, Dawn, 173
Sopranos, The, 172
"Soul Coaxing", 99
The Sound Of Music, 67
"South", 147
Southern Library Of Recorded Music (SLRM), 82, 85, 92, 95, 100, 105, 113, 115, 122, 128, 155, 162, 194
Southern Music, 33, 35, 80, 91, 95, 112, 194
Spanberger, Kathy, 148, 149, 194
Spark Records, 105, 121, 123
"Sparrow In The Tree Top", 28
Spillane, Mickey, 88
Spitalny, Phil, 17
Stafford, Jo, 139
Stanfield, Brad, 139
"Star Dust", 62

Starr, Kay, 116
Starr, Lonnie, 23, 44, 50, 73
Stealing Home, 171
Steele, Sue, 97
Steely Dan, 124
Stewart, Bill, 102, 147, 159
Stewart, Earl, 91
Stewart, Martha, 181
Stokowski, Leopold, 74
Stone, Steve, 124, 153
Strange, Michael, 44
Streisand, Barbra, 52
Sullivan, Ed, 67
"Sunshine Superman", 41
"Superman", 147, 155
Sutherland, Jimmie, 20
Sutter, Anna Ray, 32
Swing Kids, 182
Syracuse Army Air Base, 8, 10

"T For Texas", 80, 82, 138
TACET, 31
Art Tacker, 23
Taco, 159, 160
Taps, Jonie, 9
Tars And Spars, 18, 19
Taylor, Burt, 32
Thiele, Bob, 60
Thieves Like Us, 128
This Is The Army, 8, 10
Three Bells, The, 75
Tilzer, Harry Von, 2
Tin Pan Alley, 2, 29, 62
Third Rock From The Sun, 193
Tinsel Town, 155
Tiomkin, Dimitri, 73
"To Belong", 53
"There's a Party Going On", 116
"Tomorrow Is Another Day", 41
"Tomorrow Park Hill", 108
Too Much Sun, 181
"Top of the Piano", 54

Topolsky, Ken, 171
"Tossing and Turning", 76, 112
Toscanini, Arturo, 8
Travis-Chin, Edwin, 170
Triton Music, 181
Trouble In Mind, 162
Trust, Sam, 116, 153
"Two Little Angels", 53
Trade Papers, 68
Trilling, Al, 23, 72, 73
Tucker, Richard, 119
Turandot, 14

Umeki, Myoshi, 45
Universal Music, 191
University Film Association, 100
Unkel, 13

Vale, Jerry, 35, 88
Valentine, Judy, 38
Les Vegas and Billy Woods, 53, 54
The Vikings, 45, 59
Vincent, Mark, 182
Viva California, 105

"Waiting For A Train", 116
Waldo, Elizabeth, 105
WPEN, 32
WHDH, 23
"Walk Right In", 82 147
Wall Street Journal, 156
Walls of Fire, 82, 147
Walters, Barbara, 134
Wallace, Ken, 180
Waltz Time, 17, 21
Wanke, Hugh, 32
Warfield, Chris, 115, 142
Waring, Fred, 35, 62
Washington, Dinah, 77
Washington, Ned, 28
Wayne, Bernie, 33, 39
Wayne, Bobby, 40

Wayne, John, 73, 141
Watts, Robin, 63
"Wear Your Love Like Heaven", 99
Webster, Kurt, 33
Weiss, Marty, 130
Weiss, Renee, 116
Welk, Lawrence, 92, 124
Weisman, Lynn, 170
Welch, Lenny, 128
Wessel, Diane, 173
"What Good Is Somebody New", 39
"What In The World's Come Over You", 155
"When My Blue Moon Turns To Gold Again", 147
Who Do You Trust, 64
"Why Does A Woman Cry", 41, 42, 43, 52
"Wibbly Wobbly Walrus", 54
Wild, Earl, 59
Williams, Mary, 170
White, Kitty, 44
White, Steve, 46
Williams, Andy, 64, 102
Williams, Roger, 55
Williams, William B., 72
Willis Sisters, The, 79, 85, 87

Willis, Andra, 86, 93, 100, 127
Willis, Sheryl, 87
Willis, Tondea, 79, 86, 89, 97
Winchell, Danny, 33, 55, 85
Winchell, Walter, 55
"Winchester Cathedral, 91
Wise Guy, 172
Without Warning, 155
Women In Cell Block 7, 128
Wonder Years, The, 112

Yokoyama, Dr., 183
Yost, Ben, 40, 45, 55
"You Are My Sunshine", 106
"You Can Depend On Me", 76
You Gotta Walk It Like You Talk It, 123
Young Widder Brown, 40, 65
Young, Victor, 28
Youngman, Henny, 50
Your Father's Mustache, 116
You're Nobody Till Somebody Loves You, 77, 91

Zarin, Michael, 20, 21

www.ingramcontent.com/pod-product-compliance
Lightning Source LLC
Chambersburg PA
CBHW070739160426
43192CB00009B/1498